D1222968

WHAT IT
TAKES TO
WIN

Most CelebrityPress® titles are available at special quantity discounts for bulk purchases for sales promotions, premiums, fundraising, and educational use. Special versions or book excerpts can also be created to fit specific needs.

For more information, please write:
CelebrityPress®
520 N. Orlando Ave, #2
Winter Park, FL 32789
or call 1.877.261.4930

Visit us online at: www.CelebrityPressPublishing.com

WHAT IT TAKES TO
WIN

CelebrityPress®
Winter Park, Florida

CONTENTS

CHAPTER 11
WHAT IF EVERYTHING YOU KNEW ABOUT VIDEO...WAS WRONG?

CHAPTER 1

PERSIST UNTIL YOU SUCCEED

BY BRIAN TRACY

Few things are impossible to diligence and skill; great works are performed not by strength, but by perseverance.
~ Samuel Johnson

Every great success in your life will represent a triumph of persistence. Your ability to decide what you want, to begin, and then to persist through all obstacles and difficulties until you achieve your goals is the critical determinant of your success. And the flip side of persistence is courage.

Perhaps the greatest challenge that you will ever face in life is the conquest of fear and the development of the habit of courage. Winston Churchill once wrote, "Courage is rightly considered the foremost of the virtues, for, upon it, all others depend."

THE CONQUEST OF FEAR

Fear is, and always has been, the greatest enemy of mankind. When Franklin D. Roosevelt said, *"The only thing we have to fear is fear itself,"* he was saying that the *emotion* of fear, rather than the reality of what we fear, is what causes us anxiety, stress, and unhappiness.

When you (develop the habit of courage and unshakable self-confidence,) a whole new world of possibilities opens up for you. Just think – what would you dare to dream, or be, or do, if you weren't afraid of anything in the whole world?)

YOU CAN LEARN ANYTHING YOU NEED TO LEARN

Fortunately, the habit of courage can be learned just as any other success skill is learned. To do so, you need to go to work on yourself to conquer your fears, while simultaneously building up the kind of courage and confidence that will enable you to deal with the inevitable ups and downs of life unafraid.

Syndicated columnist Ann Landers wrote these words: "If I were asked to give what I consider the single most useful bit of advice for all humanity, it would be this: Expect trouble as an inevitable part of life, and when it comes, hold your head high. Look it squarely in the eye, and say, 'I will be bigger than you. You cannot defeat me.'" *This* is the kind of attitude that leads to victory.

THE CAUSES AND CURES OF FEAR

The starting point in overcoming fear and developing courage is, first of all, to look at the factors that predispose us toward being afraid. As we know, the root source of fear is childhood conditioning, usually destructive criticism from one or both parents, that causes us to experience two types of fear. These are, first of all, the fear of failure, which causes us to think, "I can't, I can't, I can't"; and second, the fear of rejection, which causes us to think, "I have to, I have to, I have to."

Because of these fears, we become preoccupied with the fears of losing our money, or our time, or our emotional investment in a relationship. We become hypersensitive to the opinions and possible criticisms of others, sometimes to the point where we are afraid to do anything that anyone else might disapprove of. Our fears tend to paralyze us, holding us back from taking constructive action in the direction of our dreams and goals. We hesitate. We become indecisive. We procrastinate. We make excuses and find reasons to delay. And finally, we feel frustrated, caught in the double bind of, "I have to, but I can't," or, "I can't, but I have to."

FEAR AND IGNORANCE GO TOGETHER

Fear can be caused by ignorance. When we have limited information, we may be tense and insecure about the outcome of our actions. Ignorance causes us to fear change, to fear the unknown and to avoid trying anything new or different.

But the reverse is also true. The very act of gathering more information and experience in a particular area gives us more courage and confidence in that area. There are parts of your life where you have no fear at all because you have mastered that area, like driving a car, skiing or selling and managing. Because of your knowledge and experience, you feel completely capable of handling whatever happens. You have no fears.

FATIGUE DOTH MAKE COWARDS OF US ALL

Another factor that causes fear is illness or fatigue. When we are tired or unwell, or when we are not physically fit, we are more predisposed to fear and doubt than when we are feeling healthy and happy and energetic.

Sometimes you can totally change your attitude toward yourself and your potential by getting a good night's sleep or taking a vacation long enough to completely recharge your mental and emotional batteries. Rest and relaxation build courage and confidence as much as any other factors.

EVERYONE IS AFRAID

Here is an important point: All intelligent people are afraid of *something.* It is normal and natural to be concerned about your physical, emotional and financial survival. The courageous person is not a person who is unafraid. As Mark Twain said, "Courage is resistance to fear, mastery of fear not absence of fear."

It is not whether or not you are afraid. We are all afraid. The question is, how do you deal with the fear? The courageous person is simply one who goes forward in spite of the fear. And here is something else I have learned: when you *confront* your fears and move toward what you are afraid of, your fears diminish while at the same time, your self-esteem and self-confidence increases.

However, when you *avoid* the thing you fear, your fears grow until they begin to control every aspect of your life. And as your fears increase, your self-esteem, your self-confidence, and your self-respect diminish accordingly. As the actor, Glenn Ford once said, "If you do not do the thing you fear, the fear controls your life."

ANALYZE YOUR FEARS

Once we have recognized the factors that can cause fear, the next step in overcoming fear is to sit down and take the time to objectively identify, define and analyze your own personal fears.

At the top of a clean sheet of paper, write the question, "What am I afraid of?"

Begin filling out your list of fears by writing down everything, major and minor, over which you experience any anxiety. Start with the most common fears, the fears of failure or loss and the fears of rejection or criticism.

Some people, dominated by the *fear of failure*, invest an enormous amount of energy justifying or covering up their mistakes. They cannot deal with the idea of making a mistake. Others, preoccupied with the *fear of rejection*, are so sensitive to how they appear to others that they seem to have no ability to take independent action at all. Until they are absolutely certain that someone else will approve, they refrain from doing anything.

SET PRIORITIES ON YOUR FEARS

Once you have made a list of every fear that you think may be affecting your thinking and your behavior, organize the items in order of importance. Which fear do you feel has the greatest impact on your thinking, or holds you back more than any other? Which fear would be number two? What would be your third fear? And so on.

With regard to your predominant fear, write the answers to these three questions:

1. How does this fear hold me back in life? *
2. How does this fear help me, or how has it helped me in the past?
3. What would be my payoff for eliminating this fear?

Some years ago, I went through this exercise and concluded that my biggest fear was the fear of poverty. I was afraid of not having enough money, being broke, perhaps even being destitute. I knew that this fear had originated during my childhood because my parents, who grew up during the Depression, had continually worried about money. My fear was reinforced when I was broke at various times during my 20's. I could objectively assess the origins of this fear, but it still had a strong hold on me. Even when I had sufficient money for all my needs, this fear was always there.

My answer to the first question, "How does this fear hold me back?" was that it caused me to be anxious about taking risks with money. It caused me to play it safe with regard to employment. And it caused me to choose security over opportunity.

My answer to the second question, "How does this fear help me?" was that, in order to escape the fear of poverty, I had developed the habit of working much longer and harder than the average person. I was more ambitious and determined. I took much more time to study and learn about the various ways that money could be made and invested. The fear of poverty was, in effect, driving me toward financial independence.

When I answered the third question, "What would be my payoff for overcoming this fear?" I immediately saw that I would be willing to take more risks, I would be more aggressive in pursuing my financial goals, I could and would start my own business, and I would not be so tense and concerned about spending too much or having too little. Especially, I would no longer be so concerned about the price of everything.

By objectively analyzing my biggest fear in this way, I was able to begin the process of eliminating it. And so can you.

PRACTICE MAKES PERMANENT

You can begin the process of developing courage and eliminating fear by engaging in actions consistent with the behaviors of courage and self-confidence. Anything that you practice over and over eventually becomes a new habit. You develop courage by behaving courageously whenever courage is called for.

Here are some of the activities you can practice to develop the habit of courage. The first and perhaps most important kind of courage is the courage to *begin*, to launch, to step out in faith. This is the courage to try something new or different, to move out of your comfort zone, with no guarantee of success.

Earlier I mentioned Professor Robert Ronstadt of Babson College who taught entrepreneurship for many years. He conducted a study of those who took his class and found that only 10% actually started their own businesses and became successful later in life. He could only find one quality that the successful graduates had in common. It was their willingness to actually start their own businesses, as opposed to continually talking about it.

THE COURAGE TO BEGIN

He discovered the "Corridor Principle," that we spoke about earlier. As these individuals moved forward toward their goals, as though proceeding down a corridor, doors opened to them that they would not have seen if they had not been in forward motion.

It turned out that the graduates of his entrepreneurship course who had done nothing with what they had learned were still waiting for things to be *just right* before they began. They were unwilling to launch themselves down the corridor of uncertainty until they could somehow be assured that they would be successful something which never happened.

THE FUTURE BELONGS TO THE RISK TAKERS

The future belongs to the *risk takers*, not the security seekers. Life is perverse in the sense that, the more you seek security, the less of it you have. But the more you seek opportunity, the more likely it is that you will achieve the security that you desire.

Whenever you feel fear or anxiety, and you need to bolster your courage to persist in the face of obstacles and setbacks, switch your attention to your goals. Create a clear mental picture of the person that you would like to be, performing the way you would like to perform. There is nothing wrong with thoughts of fear as long as you temper them with thoughts of courage and self-reliance. Whatever you dwell upon, grows . . . so be careful.

The mastery of fear and the development of courage are essential prerequisites for a happy, successful life. With a commitment to acquire the habit of courage, you will eventually reach the point where your fears no longer play a major role in your decision-making. You will set big, challenging, exciting goals, and you will have the confidence of knowing that you can attain them. You will be able to face every situation with calmness and self-assurance. And the key is courage.

LEARN FROM THE MASTERS

What if you could sit down with one of the most successful men or women in our society and learn from him or her all the lessons of success that he or she had taken a lifetime to gather? Do you think that would help you to be more successful?

What if you could sit down with 100 of the most successful men and women who ever lived and learn from their rules, their lessons and their secrets of success? Would that help you to be more successful in your own life? What if you could sit down, over time, with more than 1,000 highly successful men and women? How about 2,000 or 3,000?

ACTION IS EVERYTHING

Your answer is probably that spending time with these extremely successful men and women, learning what they learned in order to achieve their goals, would be of great help to you. The truth, however, is that all of this advice and input would do you no good at all unless you took some specific action on what you had learned.

If learning about success was all that it took to do great things with your life, then your success would be guaranteed. The bookstores are full of self-help books, each one of them loaded with ideas that you can use to be more successful. The fact is, however, that all of the best advice in the world will only help you if you can motivate yourself to take persistent, continuous action in the direction of your goals until you succeed.

The probable result of your reading the ideas in this book has been that you have made some specific decisions about things that you are going to do more of, and things that you are going to do less of. You have set certain goals for yourself in different areas of your life, and you have made resolutions that you are determined to follow through on. The most important question for your future now is simply: "Will you do what you have resolved to do?"

SELF-DISCIPLINE IS THE CORE QUALITY

The most important single quality for success is self-discipline. Self-discipline means that you have the ability, within yourself, based on your strength of character and willpower, to *"do what you should do, when you should do it, whether you feel like it or not."*

Character is the ability to follow through on a resolution after the enthusiasm with which the resolution was made has passed. It is not what you learn that is decisive for your future. It is whether or not you can put your head down and discipline yourself to pay the price, over and over, until you finally obtain your objective.

You need self-discipline in order to set your goals and to make plans for their accomplishment. You need self-discipline to continually revise and upgrade your plans with new information. You need self-discipline to use your time well and to always concentrate on the one thing, the most important thing that you need to do at the moment.

You need self-discipline to invest in yourself every day, to build yourself up personally and professionally, to learn what you need to learn in order to enjoy the success of which you are capable.

You need self-discipline to delay gratification, to save your money and to organize your finances so that you can achieve financial independence in the course of your working lifetime. You need self-discipline to keep your thoughts on your goals and dreams and keep them off of your doubts and fears. You need self-discipline to respond positively and constructively in the face of every difficulty.

PERSISTENCE IS SELF-DISCIPLINE IN ACTION

Perhaps the most important demonstration of self-discipline is your level of persistence when the going gets tough. Persistence is self-discipline in action. Persistence is the true measure of individual human character. Your persistence is, in fact, your real measure of your belief in yourself and your ability to succeed.

Each time that you persist in the face of adversity and disappointment, you build up the habit of persistence. You build pride, power, and self-esteem into your character and your personality. You become stronger and more resolute. You deepen your levels of self-discipline and personal strength. You develop in yourself the iron quality of success, the one quality that will carry you forward and over any obstacle that life can throw in your path.

THE COMMON QUALITY OF SUCCESS IN HISTORY

The history of the human race is the story of the triumph of persistence. Every great man or woman has had to endure tremendous trials and tribulations before reaching the heights of success and achievement. That endurance and perseverance are what made them great.

Winston Churchill is considered by many to have been the greatest statesman of the 20th century. Throughout his life, he was known and respected for his courage and persistence. During the darkest hours of World War II, when the German Luftwaffe was bombing Britain, and England stood alone, Churchill's resolute, bulldog tenacity inspired the whole nation to fight on in the face of what many felt was inevitable defeat. John F. Kennedy said of his speeches that, "Churchill marshaled the English language and sent it forward into battle."

One of the greatest speeches in the annals of persistence was Churchill's address to the nation on June 4th, 1940, which ended with these words, "We shall not flag or fail. We shall fight in France. We shall fight on the seas and oceans. We shall fight with growing confidence and growing strength in the air. We shall defend our islands, whatever the cost may be. We shall fight on the beaches. We shall fight on the landing grounds. We shall fight in the fields and in the streets. We shall fight in the hills; we shall never surrender."

In the later years of his life, Churchill was asked to address a class at his old preparatory school. They asked him if he would share with the young people present what he believed to be the secret of his great success in life. He stood before the assembly, leaning on his cane, shaking a little, and said with a strong voice, "I can summarize the lessons of my life in seven words: never give in; never, never give in."

YOUR GUARANTEE OF EVENTUAL SUCCESS

What Churchill found, and what you will discover as you move upward and onward toward your goals, is that persistence is the one quality that guarantees that you will eventually win through.

Calvin Coolidge, a President who was so reluctant to speak in public that he was given the nickname of "Silent Cal," will go down in history for his simple but memorable words on this subject. He wrote: *"Press on. Nothing in the world can take the place of persistence. Talent will not; nothing is more common than unsuccessful men with talent. Genius will not; unrewarded genius is almost a proverb. Education alone will not; the world is full of educated derelicts. Persistence and determination alone are omnipotent."*

PERSISTENCE IS THE HALLMARK OF SUCCESS

Successful business people and entrepreneurs are all characterized by indomitable willpower and unshakable persistence.

In 1895, America was in the grip of a terrible depression. A man living in the Midwest lost his hotel in the midst of this depression and decided to write a book to motivate and inspire others to persist and carry on in spite of the difficulties facing the nation.

His name was Orison Swett Marden. He took a room above a livery stable, and for an entire year, he worked night and day writing a book, which he entitled *Pushing To The Front*. Late one evening, he finally finished the last page of his book and, being tired and hungry, he went down the street to a small café for dinner. While he was away for an hour, the livery stable caught on fire, and by the time he got back, his entire manuscript, more than 800 pages, had been destroyed by the flames.

Nonetheless, drawing on his inner resources, he sat down and spent another year writing the book over again from scratch. When the book was finished, he offered it to various publishers, but no one seemed to be interested in a motivational book with the country in such a depression and unemployment so high. He then moved to Chicago and took another job. One day he mentioned this manuscript to a friend of his who happened to know a publisher. The book, *Pushing to the Front* was subsequently published and became a runaway bestseller in the nation.

Pushing To The Front was acclaimed by the leading businesspeople and politicians in America as being the book that brought America into the 20th century. It exerted an enormous impact on the minds of decision-makers throughout the country and became the greatest single classic in all of personal development.

People like Henry Ford, Thomas Edison, Harvey Firestone, and J. P. Morgan all read this book and were inspired by it.

THE TWO ESSENTIAL QUALITIES

Orison Swett Marden says in his book that, "There are two essential requirements for success. The first is 'get-to-it-iveness,' and the second is 'stick-to-it-iveness.'" He wrote, *"No, there is no failure for the man who realizes his power, who never knows when he is beaten; there is no failure for the determined endeavor; the unconquerable will. There is no failure for the man who gets up every time he falls, who rebounds like a rubber ball, who persists when everyone else gives up, who pushes on when everyone else turns back."*

Confucius said, more than 4,000 years ago, *"Our greatest glory is not in never falling, but in rising every time we fall."*

James J. Corbett, one of the first world heavyweight boxing champions, said that *"You become a champion by fighting one more round. When things are tough, you fight one more round."* Yogi Berra said this, *"It's not over until it's over."* And the fact is that it's never over as long as you continue to persist.

Elbert Hubbard wrote, *"There is no failure except in no longer trying. There is no defeat except from within, no really insurmountable barrier save our own inherent weakness of purpose."*

Vince Lombardi said, *"It's not whether you get knocked down. It's whether you get up again."*

All of these successful men and women had learned how critical the quality of persistence is in achieving greater goals and objectives. Successful men and women are hallmarked by their incredible persistence, by their refusal to quit, no matter what the external circumstances. The one quality that absolutely guarantees success in business, in financial accumulation, and in life is this indomitable willpower and the willingness to stick at it when everything in you wants to stop and rest or go back and do something else.

PERSISTENCE IS YOUR GREATEST ASSET

Perhaps your greatest asset is simply your ability to keep at it longer than anyone else. B. C. Forbes, the founder of *Forbes* Magazine, who built it into a major publication during the darkest days of the depression, wrote, "History has demonstrated that the most notable winners usually encountered heartbreaking obstacles before they triumphed. They won because they refused to become discouraged by their defeat."

John D. Rockefeller, at one time the richest self-made man in the world, wrote, *"I do not think there is any other quality so essential to success of any kind, as the quality of perseverance. It overcomes almost everything, even nature."*

Conrad Hilton, who started with a dream and a small hotel in Lubbock, Texas, and went on to build one of the most successful hotel corporations in the world, said, *"Success seems to be connected with action. Successful men keep moving. They make mistakes, but they don't quit."*

Thomas Edison, the greatest *failure*, and also the greatest success, in the history of invention, failed at more experiments than any other inventor of the 20th century. He also perfected and was granted more patents for commercial processes than any other inventor of his age. He described his philosophy in these words: *"When I have fully decided that a result is worth getting, I go ahead on it and make trial after trial until it comes. Nearly every man who develops an idea works it up to the point where it looks impossible and then gets discouraged. That's not the place to become discouraged."*

Alexander Graham Bell talked about persistence in these words, *"What this power is I cannot say; all I know is that it exists and it becomes available only when a man is in that state of mind in which he knows exactly what he wants and is fully determined not to quit until he finds it."*

Rene McPhearson, who built Dana Corporation into one of the great American success stories, summarized his philosophy by saying, *"You just keep pushing. You just keep pushing. I made every mistake that could be made, but I just kept pushing."*

THE GREAT PARADOX

There is an interesting and important paradox in life that you need to be aware of. It is that if you are an intelligent person, you do everything possible to organize your life in such a way that you minimize and avoid adversity and disappointment. This is a sensible and rational thing to do. All intelligent people, following the path of least resistance to achieve their goals, do everything possible to minimize the number of difficulties and obstacles that they will face in their day-to-day activities.

DISAPPOINTMENT IS INEVITABLE

Yet, in spite of our best efforts, disappointments and adversity are normal and natural, unavoidable parts of life. Benjamin Franklin said that the only things that are inevitable are death and taxes, but every bit of experience shows that disappointment is also inevitable. No matter how well you organize yourself and your activities, you will experience countless disappointments, setbacks, obstacles and adversity over the course of your life. And the higher and more challenging the goals that you set for yourself, the more disappointment and adversity you will experience.

This is the paradox. It is impossible for us to evolve and grow and develop to our full potentials except to the degree to which we face adversity and learn from it. All of the great lessons of life come as the result of setbacks and temporary defeats which we have done our utmost to avoid. Adversity, therefore, comes unbidden, in spite of our best efforts. And yet without it, we cannot grow into the kind of people who are capable of scaling the heights and achieving great goals.

ADVERSITY IS WHAT TESTS US

Throughout history, great thinkers have reflected on this paradox and have concluded that adversity is the test that you must pass on the path to accomplishing anything worthwhile. Herodotus, the Greek philosopher, said, *"Adversity has the effect of drawing out strength and qualities of a man that would have lain dormant in its absence."*

The very best qualities of strength, courage, character, and persistence are brought out in you when you face your greatest challenges and you respond to them positively and constructively. Everyone faces difficulties every step of the way. The difference between the high achiever and the low achiever is simply that the high achiever utilizes adversity and struggles for growth, while the low achiever allows difficulties and adversity to overwhelm him or her and leave him or her discouraged and dejected.

BOUNCE BACK FROM DISAPPOINTMENT

The work by Abraham Zaleznik at Harvard proved that the way you respond to disappointment is usually an accurate predictor of how likely you are to achieve great success. If you respond to disappointment by learning the very most from it and then by putting it behind you and pressing forward, you are very likely to accomplish great things in the course of your life.

SUCCESS COMES ONE STEP BEYOND FAILURE

This is another remarkable discovery. Your greatest successes almost invariably come one step beyond when everything inside of you says to quit. Men and women throughout history have been amazed to find that their great breakthroughs came about as a result of persisting in the face of all disappointment and all evidence to the contrary. This final act of persistence, which is often called the "persistence test," seems to precede great achievements of all kinds.

H. Ross Perot, who started EDP Industries with $1,000 and who built it into a fortune of almost three billion dollars, is one of the most successful self-made entrepreneurs in American history. He said this; *"Most people give up just when they are about to achieve success. They quit on the one-yard line. They give up at the last minute of the game, one foot away from the winning touchdown."*

Herodotus also wrote, *"Some men give up their designs when they have almost reached the goal; while others, on the contrary, obtain a victory by exerting, at the last moment, more vigorous efforts than ever before."*

You find this principle of persistence, of keeping on, in the life and work of countless great men and women. Florence Scovel Shinn wrote that *"Every great work, every big accomplishment, has been brought into manifestation through holding to the vision, and often just before the big achievement comes apparent failure and discouragement."*

Napoleon Hill, in his classic, *Think and Grow Rich*, wrote, *"Before success comes in any man's life, he is sure to meet with much temporary defeat and, perhaps, some failure. When defeat overtakes a man, the easiest and most logical thing to do is quit. And that is exactly what the majority of men and women do."*

Harriet Beecher Stowe, who wrote the *Battle Hymn of the Republic*, also wrote these words, *"Never give up then, for that is just the place and time that the tide will turn."*

What you do not see - what most people never suspect of existing - is the silent but irresistible power which comes to your rescue when you fight on in the face of discouragement.

Claude M. Bristol wrote, *"It's the constant and determined effort that breaks down all resistance, sweeps away all obstacles."*

James Whitcome Riley put it this way, *"The most essential factor is persistence - the determination never to allow your energy or enthusiasm to be dampened by the discouragement that must inevitably come."*

The power to hold on, in spite of everything, to endure - this is the winner's quality. Persistence is the ability to face defeat again and again without giving up – to push on in the face of great difficulty. There is a poem by an anonymous author that I think everyone should read and memorize and recite to himself or herself when tempted to quit or to stop trying. This poem is called *Don't Quit.*

Don't Quit

When things go wrong, as they sometimes will,
When the road you're trudging seems all uphill,
When the funds are low and the debts are high
And you want to smile, but you have to sigh,
When care is pressing you down a bit,
Rest, if you must, but don't you quit.

Life is queer with its twists and turns,
As every one of us sometimes learns,
And many a failure turns about
When he might have won had he stuck it out.
Don't give up though the pace seems slow,
You may succeed with another blow.

Success is failure turned inside out –
The silver tint of the clouds of doubt,
And you never can tell how close you are,
It may be near when it seems so far;
So, stick to the fight when you're hardest hit –
It's when things seem worst that you must not QUIT.

PERSIST UNTIL YOU SUCCEED:

1. Identify the biggest challenge or problem facing you today on the way to achieving your biggest goal. Imagine that it has been sent to test your resolve and desire. Decide that you will never give up.

2. Think back over your life and identify the occasions where your determination to persist was the key to your success. Remind yourself of those experiences whenever you face difficulties or discouragement of any kind.

3. Resolve in advance that, as long as you intensely desire your goal, you will never give up until you achieve it.

4. Look into every problem, difficulty, obstacle or setback for the seed of an equal or greater benefit or opportunity. You will always find something that can help you.

5. In every situation, resolve to be solution oriented and action-oriented. Think always in terms of the things you can do right now to solve your problems or achieve your goals, and then get started! Never give up.

SUMMARY

Take Action Today

You have now learned perhaps the most comprehensive strategy for setting and achieving goals that has ever been put together in one book. By practicing these rules and principles, you can accomplish more in the coming months and years than most people accomplish in a lifetime.

The most important quality you can develop for lifelong success is the habit of taking action on your plans, goals, ideas, and insights. The more often you try, the sooner you will triumph. There is a direct relationship between the number of things you attempt and your accomplishments in life.

Here are the 21 steps for setting and achieving goals, and for living a wonderful life:

1. **Unlock Your Potential** - Always remember that your true potential is unlimited. Whatever you have accomplished in life up to now has only been a preparation for the amazing things you can accomplish in the future.

2. **Take Charge of Your Life** - You are completely responsible for everything you are today, for everything you think, say and do, and for everything you become from this moment forward. Refuse to make excuses or to blame others. Instead, make progress toward your goals every day.

3. **Create Your Own Future** - Imagine that you have no limitations on what you can do, be or have in the months and years ahead. Think about and plan your future as if you had all the resources you needed to create any life that you desire.

4. **Clarify Your Values** - Your innermost values and convictions define you as a person. Take the time to think through what you really believe in and care about in each

area of your life. Refuse to deviate from what you feel is right for you.

5. **Determine Your True Goals** - Decide for yourself what you really want to accomplish in every area of your life. Clarity is essential for happiness and high-performance living.

6. **Decide Upon Your Major Definite Purpose** - You need a central purpose to build your life around. There must be a single goal that will help you to achieve your other goals more than any other. Decide what it is for you and work on it all the time.

7. **Analyze Your Beliefs** - Your beliefs about your own abilities, and about the world around you, will have more of an impact on your feelings and actions than any other factor. Make sure that your beliefs are positive and consistent with achieving everything that is possible for you.

8. **Start At The Beginning** - Do a careful analysis of your starting point before you set off toward the achievement of your goal. Determine your exact situation today and be both honest and realistic about what you want to accomplish in the future.

9. **Measure Your Progress** - Set clear benchmarks, measures, metrics and scorecards for yourself on the road to your goals. These measures help you to assess how well you are doing and enable you to make necessary adjustments and corrections as you go along.

10. **Eliminate The Roadblocks** - Success boils down to the ability to solve problems and remove obstacles on the path to your goal. Fortunately, problem-solving is a skill you can master with practice, and thereby achieve your goals faster than you ever thought possible.

11. **Become An Expert In Your Field** - You have within you, right now, the ability to be one of the very best at what you do, to join the top 10% in your field. Set this as a goal, work on it every day, and never stop working at it until you get there.

12. **Get Around The Right People** - Your choices of people with whom to live, work and socialize will have more of an effect on your success than any other factor. Resolve today to associate only with people you like, respect and admire. Fly with the eagles if you want to be an eagle yourself.

13. **Make a Plan Of Action** - An ordinary person with a well thought-out plan will run circles around a genius without one. Your ability to plan and organize in advance will enable you to accomplish even the biggest and most complex goals.

14. **Manage Your Time Well** - Learn how to double and triple your productivity, performance, and output by practicing practical and proven time management principles. Always set priorities before you begin, and then concentrate on the most valuable use of your time.

15. **Review Your Goals Regularly** - Take time every day, every week, every month to review and reevaluate your goals and objectives. Make sure that you are still on track and that you are still working toward things that are important to you. Be prepared to modify your goals and plans with new information.

16. **Visualize Your Goals Continually** - Direct the movies of your mind. Your imagination is the preview of your life's coming attractions. Repeatedly "see" your goals as if they already existed. Your clear, exciting mental images activate all your mental powers and attract your goals into your life.

17. **Activate Your Superconscious Mind** - You have within you and around you an incredible power that will bring you everything and anything you want or need. Take the time regularly to tap into this amazing source of ideas and insights for goal attainment.

18. **Remain Flexible At All Times** - Be clear about your goal but be flexible about the process of achieving it. Be constantly open to new, better, faster, cheaper ways to achieve the same result, and if something is not working, be willing to try a different approach.

19. **Unlock Your Inborn Creativity** - You have more creative ability to solve problems and come up with new and better ways for goal attainment than you have ever used. You are a potential genius. You can tap into your intelligence to overcome any obstacle and achieve any goal you can set for yourself.

20. **Do Something Every Day** - Use the "Momentum Principle of Success" by getting started toward your goal and then doing something every day that moves you closer to what you want to accomplish. Action orientation is essential to your success.

21. **Persist Until You Succeed** - In the final analysis, your ability to persist longer than anyone else is the one quality that will guarantee great success in life. Persistence is self-discipline in action and is the true measure of your belief in yourself. Resolve in advance that you will never, never give up!

There they are, the twenty-one most important principles of goal setting and goal achieving ever discovered. Your regular review and practice of these principles will enable you to live an extraordinary life. Nothing can stop you now.

Good luck!

About Brian

Brian Tracy is one of the top business experts and trainers in the world. He has taught more than 5,000,000 sales people in 80 countries.

He is the President of Brian Tracy International, committed to teaching ambitious individuals how to rapidly increase their sales and personal incomes.

CHAPTER 2

YOU...
THE THOUGHTLEADER®
IN YOUR FIELD!

BY JW DICKS AND NICK NANTON

Ten years ago, Nick Nanton and I founded *The Dicks+Nanton Celebrity Branding Agency* focused on the concept of *Celebrity Branding You...* How to become the Leading Exert in Your Field.

We brought to business owners and professionals concepts like, "People Buy People" and taught how to get prospects to buy you over your competitor by getting them to know, like and trust you. The fastest, easiest way to do that was to become the expert in your field, no mater what field you were in. We taught our clients the way to establish yourself as the expert was to write articles in your field, becoming a Best-Selling Author® on your topic, get on TV and be interviewed, and in general provide good valuable content to your targeted customer.

This methodology of building a business based around expert status wasn't being talked about much back then, but times have changed. Today, more than ever, people want good, authoritative content from someone they recognize as the ThoughtLeader® in the field.

We launched the Agency with our book, (following our own advice on producing content), Celebrity Branding You, followed over the years by *StorySelling* and *Mission-Driven*, (all Best-Sellers). The information in the books were supplemented by articles, websites, emails, seminars and Facebook, and with each new media available, we tried to incorporate the latest strategies in them to reach our audience.

Along the way, we attracted 3,021 clients in 65 countries, while helping clients to become Best-Selling Authors® and TV Guests, obtaining magazine appearances, and producing major Emmy award-winning documentaries about successful people sharing their knowledge and non-profits changing people's lives in other ways.

As fun and exciting as these last ten years have been, the next ten years will offer us new opportunities to have a bigger impact in peoples lives and their business. Many of our early teaching concepts have become mainstream. The world is moving much faster and the thirst for new ideas has moved from desire to desperation in many cases.

Information, and technology have blended together and the pace today is even faster.

There is also a greater need for the next level expert to lead his/ her field with new ideas and applications. More and more we are seeing the rise of the ThoughtLeader®, the next generation of Experts that people in every field of endeavor look for to provide a faster road for their own success.

But what exactly is a ThoughtLeader®?
How do you become one? Do you even want to be one?

These are the questions we will address while showing you the way to become a ThoughtLeader yourself.

CONTENT MARKETING VS. THOUGHTLEADER®

In many ways, content marketing and Thought Leadership work together.

Content marketing has become a leading way to reach your prospect or customer. It is different from traditional advertising methods. Instead of brash ads yelling how good you are, content marketing is a methodology of attracting your market's attention with good solid information that your customers are seeking from a reliable source that saves them time, money and effort required to find answers themselves.

By providing good, reliable content, people seek out the provider of this information as the Expert they could believe in to provide this information, and this creates a stronger bond of trust between the consumer and the provider of the desired content.

A ThoughtLeader® often provides original content of this type to a certain market, but he is also known for providing changing ideas, and unique insights about the direction of the topic or the field of endeavor. In many ways, the ThoughtLeader® looks beyond the surface and "sees" new ways of using traditional ideas in a field, and may also borrow ideas from other fields – adapting them to the current field they are in or morphing into something new and different.

Elon Musk for example, is clearly a ThoughtLeader in multiple fields. From automotive (Tesla), to solar (Solar City), to space travel (SpaceX), Musk's mind moves in and out from seemingly different worlds and he joins them in sort of a cross pollination, where the answers to the needs of Tesla may be borrowed from something learned in Solar City's energy farms or SpaceX rocket launches.

Peter Diamandis, one of today's leading edge ThoughtLeaders in multiple fields, was the subject of one of our documentaries entitled, *Visioneer.* The movie told of Peter's creation of The XPrize, a non-profit organization Peter founded to fund the answers to some of the world's greatest problems. In a few short years, Peter has attracted funding for the XPrizes by leading philanthropists and major corporations—offering multimillion-dollar prizes to teams of engineers and adventurers—racing each other competitively to be the first to solve the answers and win the prizes. Along the way, Peter has founded or co-founded other multimillion-dollar ventures in human longevity, asteroid mining, AI, and Singularity University, all dedicated to bold ventures for the good of mankind.

And as great as these ThoughtLeaders are, they are only "super examples" that everyone knows, yet no more important in idea development than Albert Manero, an engineering student at UCF in 2014 who created a low-priced robotic arm and 3-D printed them for a fraction of their previous cost, making them available to an entirely new and different market.

The ThoughtLeader® today can be an Expert in any field, or as we just noted, in multiple fields. In many cases, the ThoughtLeaders® can't help themselves to provide information and ideas to others, "its just what they do."

The ThoughtLeader® becomes the source of knowledge in a field. They help people sort through the content to determine truth or fiction – to help consumers find answers to their questions from an authoritative source they are confident in and trust. Once that ThoughtLeader status is formally or informally bestowed on someone, it is a very powerful element of trust that is hard to break up. The bond created encourages the customer to shift to the ThoughtLeaders® for other products or services provided as an exchange of value to each other.

ThoughtLeadership is also more than just information providing. It also is a smart business strategy to develop at any level of business.

Just as IBM uses its computer, Watson, to grow its Cognitive Business strategy, it also uses it as a method of bringing IBM into large businesses that want information on cloud computing and data analytics. By being the Thoughtleader® in these fields though its Watson technologies, IBM is always in the conversation when companies talk about them and look for someone to provide high-level services.

IBM may not always get every contract in these fields, but a company would be making a mistake not to at least consider them when looking for this type of service. "After all," a buyer would tell his board of directors... "IBM is the leader in this field."

What does this business lesson teach you about using Thought Leadership as a strategic advantage in your field?

Forester's Laura Ramos says Thought Leadership impacts business at each and every stage of the buying journey: "... we have found companies benefit from it in the early stage... through more inbound inquiries and short listing for contracts; in the middle stage... through faster sales cycles, higher close rates, and bigger deal sizes; and in the late stage... through increased customer loyalty and higher lifetime value!"[1]

In our own business with thousand of clients, we have seen various levels of embracement of Thought Leadership as a business strategy. Clearly, the clients who "get it" and continue to position themselves in this ThoughtLeader® role, supplying a continuing flow of authority content to its customer base, is rewarded by more business from its existing customer base. Additionally, the business process becomes a new marketing strategy that brings in new customers who are looking for answers from authoritative figures who freely provide answers to their questions.

1. http://blogs.forrester.com/laura_ramos/13-09-11-thought_leadership_hot _topic_at_cs_forum_helsinki_2013. (See Footnote References at end of chapter)

This new relationship between customer and ThoughtLeader® must, like all business relationships, be continually reinforced or others will take the ThoughtLeader's place in this highly competitive marketplace.

From a strategic standpoint, the ThoughtLeader® must continue to maintain a position in the minds of their customer, through a never-ending stream of top-level information in their field. This is certainly done through email, but it also must be done through other avenues of delivery such as blogs, articles, newsletters, books and video. It is not a one-and-done strategy. It is work to maintain any relationship, and the same is true with customers who are busy with their own lives, while you are popping in and out with information they want.

The difference between ThoughtLeader® strategy and hit-and-run advertising and marketing is that the strategy is long-term. Each month you follow the strategy you are building on the previous month, and your relationship with the customer is stronger. They begin to rely rely on you for the information they need and that begins to create a level of trust.

WHAT TYPE OF INFORMATION DO YOU PROVIDE AS A THOUGHTLEADER®?

As you might guess, this is a very important question that many people don't get.

A ThoughtLeader® provides information that their customers want. It's ALL ABOUT THE CUSTOMER!

Forget that message and you are lost. I don't care how good your content is, if it isn't the type of content your customers want, they will lose interest and you will lose a customer. It is very important for you to understand this. The more you vary from the message that brought you the customer, the greater the chance you have of losing them.

If you are a financial planner and your customer was attracted to you because you talked about boomer retirement strategies, you continue to make that your message. The moment you start talking about the financial programs good for the millennial, the faster you will lose the attention of the boomer. Yes, you can create a separate educational track and segment markets but that is very difficult to do and requires double everything content-wise, including another targeted web site.

Think about Dave Ramsey. Dave is known for his debt-free, financial planning approach to your finances. He has talked about the same approach for years and doesn't vary his message. He continues to keep his listeners who were first attracted by this message and he gets new listeners who are attracted for the first time.

Does Dave's message get tiring sometimes? Maybe, just as we tire sometimes of a favorite song. But then when we hear it again, it awakens a sense that had paused for a moment and the good feeling comes back again. So it is in your business market and every market. The art is to try and keep the information timely but consistent; all the great ones do it no matter what the industry. It is even true in politics, and you only have to look at Donald Trump and see the lesson applied to politics. Like him or not, the President stays on message. His buyers, (his voters), never tire of what he has to say and they keep tuned in to the same message. So will your customers.

BUILDING YOUR THOUGHTLEADER® PLATFORM

To be a successful ThoughtLeader®, you must have a platform. It is your home base from where you operate. Dave Ramsey's main platform is his nationally-syndicated radio show. He does have a website, books he has written and other platforms (such as Facebook), but his main platform is his radio show. Without the radio show he would not have the recognition that he has. Unfortunately, reality sets in when I tell you that at first it is very unlikely you will have a national radio show as your platform when you first start out, and neither did Dave Ramsey. In most cases, your platform will be your website as you build your reputation as a ThoughtLeader in your field.

The good news is that good productive websites have fallen in cost the past couple of years and they tend to be less complex. All of this really depends on your budget, but if you don't have a website your business will be severly handicapped.

Your website should convey very quickly who you are, what you do, and how you can help. Remember, earlier we talked about your content being more about the customer and less about you. This is also true about your platform website … more customer driven and less "you" driven.

This does not mean you don't have a great photo of yourself, because you must have a good one. People still react to people and a good photo with your smile is important for your guest to feel comfortable with you.

You will also share information about yourself. But the best way to do that is through testimonials of your customers. Let them brag on you. The more credibility they have, the better for you. In the beginning, get testimonials from whomever you can. As your business grows and you have bigger customers, let them talk for you and the message will be received much better.

While I could go on and on about how to build your Platform Website, the best information I can give you is to go to one of my partners and my daughter, Lindsay's website at CelebritySites. com. What she has forgotten about websites and SEO is more than I know, and she has lots of free information that you can get and use when interviewing a Webmaster, or as a checklist if you are able to build your own.

The point about platform websites from my perspective is that a successful ThoughtLeader® must have a great platform to launch your content from and connect with your audience. Spend the time, money and effort to get it right. You will be glad you did. Please feel free to also go to our website for more content on building your business, and on your professional position as the expert and ThoughtLeader® in your field.

Footnote 1 – References
(a). The Sophisticated Marketers Guide to Thought Leadership, LinkedIn. Jason Miller, Group Manager, Global Content and Social Media Marketing, LinkedIn Marketing Solutions
(b). http://blogs.forrester.com/laura_ramos/13-09-11-thought_ leadership_ hot_topic_at_cs_forum_helsinki_2013

About JW

JW Dicks, Esq., is a Business Development Attorney, a *Wall Street Journal* Best-Selling Author—who has authored over 47 books—and a 2x Emmy Award-Winning Executive Producer.

JW is an XPrize Innovation Board member, Chairman of the Board of the National Academy of Best-Selling Authors®, Board Member of the National Association of Experts, Writers and Speakers® and Board Member of the International Academy of Film Makers®.

JW is the CEO of DNAgency, an Inc. 5000 Multi Media Company that represents over 3,000 clients in 65 countries. He has been quoted on business and financial topics in national media such as *USA Today, The Wall Street Journal, Newsweek, Forbes, CNBC.com*, and *Fortune Magazine Small Business.*

Considered a ThoughtLeader® and curator of information, JW has co-authored books with legends like Jack Canfield, Brian Tracy, Tom Hopkins, Dr. Nido Qubein, Steve Forbes, Richard Branson, Michael Gerber, Dr. Ivan Misner, and Dan Kennedy. He is the Publisher of *ThoughtLeader® Magazine.*

JW is called the "Expert to the Experts" and has appeared on business television shows airing on ABC, NBC, CBS, and FOX affiliates around the country and coproduces and syndicates a line of franchised business television shows such as *Success Today, Wall Street Today, Hollywood Live,* and *Profiles of Success.*

JW and his wife of forty-seven years, Linda, have two daughters, four granddaughters and two Yorkies. He is a sixth-generation Floridian and splits his time between his home in Orlando and his beach house on Florida's west coast.

About Nick

An Emmy Award-Winning Director and Producer, Nick Nanton, Esq., produces media and branded content for top thought leaders and media personalities around the world. Recognized as a leading expert on branding and storytelling, Nick has authored more than two dozen Best-Selling books (including the *Wall Street Journal* Best-Seller, *StorySelling*™) and produced and directed more than 50 documentaries, earning 5 Emmy wins and 18 nominations. Nick speaks to audiences internationally on the topics of branding, entertainment, media, business and storytelling at major universities and events.

As the CEO of DNA Media, Nick oversees a portfolio of companies including: The Dicks + Nanton Agency (an international agency with more than 3000 clients in 65 countries), Dicks + Nanton Productions, Ambitious.com and DNA Films. Nick is an award-winning director, producer and songwriter who has worked on everything from large scale events to television shows with the likes of Steve Forbes, Ivanka Trump, Sir Richard Branson, Rudy Ruettiger (inspiration for the Hollywood Blockbuster, *RUDY*), Brian Tracy, Jack Canfield *(The Secret*, creator of the *Chicken Soup for the Soul* Series), Michael E. Gerber, Tom Hopkins, Dan Kennedy and many more.

Nick has been seen in *USA Today, The Wall Street Journal, Newsweek, BusinessWeek, Inc. Magazine, The New York Times, Entrepreneur*® *Magazine, Forbes* and *Fast Company*, and has appeared on ABC, NBC, CBS, and FOX television affiliates across the country, as well as on CNN, FOX News, CNBC, and MSNBC coast-to-coast.

Nick is a member of the Florida Bar, a member of The National Academy of Television Arts & Sciences (Home to the EMMYs), co-founder of The National Academy of Best-Selling Authors®, and serves on the Innovation Board of the XPRIZE Foundation, a non-profit organization dedicated to bringing about "radical breakthroughs for the benefit of humanity" through incentivized competition and best known for its Ansari XPRIZE—which incentivized the first private space flight and was the catalyst for Richard Branson's *Virgin Galactic*. Nick also enjoys serving as an Elder at Orangewood Church, working with Young Life, Downtown Credo Orlando, Entrepreneurs International and rooting for the Florida Gators with his wife Kristina and their three children,

Brock, Bowen and Addison.

Learn more at:
- www.NickNanton.com
- www.CelebrityBrandingAgency.com

CHAPTER 3

SEVEN SECRETS TO DERIVE HIGHER VALUATION FOR YOUR SMALL OR MEDIUM ENTERPRISE

BY RAJASRI SRISKANDARAJAH

"How much is my business is worth?"

This seems to be a question every entrepreneur stumbles upon at some point in their career. However, it is typically considered too late and does not inspire the needed constructive thought process to flow for an effective valuation of a business. It is the job of the entrepreneur to ask questions or seek the necessary support to effectively derive a higher valued company:

1) What needs to be changed to increase the value of my business?
2) How am I ahead of the competition?
3) Is this a sustainable and efficient way of running my business?
4) What are our strengths? What about our weaknesses?

5) What is the evidence or data that will justify a higher valuation? This includes, but is not limited to, details such as published data on market potentials and sustainability of the business and its revenues.

Questioning yourself and seeking advice is always a good start, but the key to a business with a higher valuation follows implementation of basic principles and formulas.

Why valuation is important
There are many goals for a successful business; the primary one is money-making. If you do the right thing and work towards a better business, money will flow in on its own. So why do people evaluate their net worth?

It allows you to have an idea of where you stand and provides insight as to how much leeway others may offer you. This can tell you the level of trust investors may have in you, or the size of loans you are allowed to withdraw from a financial institute.

Unfortunately, the valuation process is most commonly done when the owner plans to move on from the business. Should the owner decide to hand the business over to loved ones, having a concrete numerical value helps with the division of the business. If the owner is selling, they should know the ideal price to sell to maximize their income, and implement the appropriate tax plans to minimize their taxes.

VALUATION METHOD

There are no set rules available for company valuation. I would like to point out that modern-day companies such as Tesla are valued at levels that are difficult to understand; while they are in debt with no profits made and not having a clear succession plan compared to the traditional automotive companies, proves a point to this fact.

However, the most common valuation method is to use the following formula:

Factor x Earnings Before Interest, Taxes, Depreciation, and Amortization (EBITDA)

The factor will be determined based on your industry, goodwill, intellectual property, the company's physical location and others. EBITDA is derived from the financial statements.

Some individuals have constructed the idea that altering financial statements before valuation will increase the value of their company. This is a misconception and a mistake that professionals in the valuation industry will quickly latch onto. Following proper business management techniques fosters a company's growth. In this chapter, my aim is to provide you with my seven primary practical tips to enhance the value of your small or medium-sized enterprise.

1. Numbers tell your story

When dealing with bankers or investors, financial statements are required to summarize your business' unique positioning and performance using various ratios. Understanding the ratios on the financial statements and the reasons behind them is the first step to knowing your company. In this chapter, my aim is to touch the primary points to give an idea what to look for.

To most business owners, as the company grows and business becomes complex, knowing details of your finances can become very challenging.

- **Financial statements and reporting systems**
  When a business is small, owners themselves can control the whole operation with annual financial statements that are prepared primarily for tax purposes and for financing arrangements.

As the company grows, financial information is now used for internal control and management reporting. Not only that, but third parties such as banks, investors, and boards of directors will now require reports on a monthly or quarterly basis as the bank facilities are increased. Planning well in advance with an expert in the field may be a smart decision.

- **Costing and pricing models**
  Cost models are the basis of how your products and services are priced, and it will impact your profitability. Product, price, promotion, and place will drive the company's sales volume, and in turn, your market share.

  Many companies use a method known as standard costing to plan their ideal prices. These models are created from a budget that considers labour, overhead absorption rates, efficiency, and capacity. These rates are used in allocating resources while deriving the cost of a product. During the production and sales phase, the actual numbers are compared to the created budget numbers to identify the variance. It is vital to monitor the deviations on a regular basis and to take corrective action if necessary for continuous improvement.

2. Make your balance sheet strong

- **Do not dry the reserves**
  Be sure to always have cash reserves for rainy days. A good retained earnings account on your balance sheet indicates that the business has been profitable and is healthy.

- **Reinvesting is crucial**
  With the changes in economic conditions, sometimes money may be tight, and at other times your business may be thriving. In either case, one of the significant

mistakes business owners can make to stop investing in the company. Not reinvesting hinders the growth and future value of the company.

3. Prepare a structured strategic plan with smart goals

All companies need to aspire for a bright future. They need to know what their short and long-term goals are, and steps they will take to achieve these goals.

At all levels of the company, people should be challenged with SMART goals:
- Specific
- Measurable
- Attainable
- Relevant
- Time-bound

The purpose of these goals is to keep the company relevant in the market. If the company is unable to keep ahold of their own preset goals, it is unlikely that it can keep up with usual standards.

A good starting point is to understand your mission and vision, to develop the goals and objectives that you would like to achieve, and to critically analyze your strengths, weakness, opportunities, and threats (SWOT). A SWOT allows businesses to evaluate themselves and their competition, so that they can exploit your strengths and minimize your weaknesses to harness your opportunities while limiting their risks.

In doing a SWOT analysis, businesses can:

- Identify the most demanding internal and external challenges. It is important to assess where you are to determine what changes need to follow to meet your goals and objectives.

- Evaluate opportunities for alternatives and think outside the box to grab new market opportunities, new technologies, products or services, in order to solve customer needs. For example: what will make us lose market share or experience unexpected competition and disruptive technology? Look at how the film, media, and music industries have changed over the years – from records to tapes to CDs to USBs to the cloud.
- Strategically scale and validate the business ideas that will generate maximum benefits and create a competitive advantage.

4. Build Your Brand and Goodwill

In today's environment, branding has evolved due to social media. One simple mistake can ruin the image that was built over many years. Following are the fundamental principles that will keep the company's name in good standing:

- **Customers are those whom we serve**
  The public associates a brand with quality versus expectations. Whatever business you are in, you can never go wrong by treating your customers right. In doing so, they will psychologically follow the mere exposure effect; that is, they will appreciate you more because they are not only familiar with the brand, your products and service, but also enjoy the experience and are happy or proud of associating with your brand.

- **Honesty is the best policy**
  Honesty and communication are the best policies in brand building. Lying to customers is one of the biggest mistakes you can make. Behind every business are people and people make mistakes, which is understandable and forgivable. Problems arise when one of two things happen:

    a. The company attempts to cover up the mistake

    b. The company admits to their mistakes but does not take a proactive approach to resolve the issue

- **Social responsibility**
  Embrace corporate social responsibility (CSR). It is a company's primary responsibility to satisfy their main stakeholders: customers, employees, owners, and the environment. Successful entrepreneurs believe that businesses should give back to society.

5. Automated and scalable processes

In today's electronic world, business models and systems should be designed with automation; it is now an expectation rather than a luxury to offer a sense of availability 24/7. In today's era of online bookings, orders, and payments, use of up-to-date technology is a necessity.

In recent days, people have been able to integrate technology into industries where it was believed that machines could not replace people. An example would be the medical field; although computers cannot replace doctors and nurses, electronic medical records, robotic operating theatres, and computer-aided diagnostic systems are becoming vital equipment pieces that doctors require for efficiencies.

This brings a valuable perspective of out-of-the-box thinking: how will people assimilate the use of technology in the future? Think about where we started, and where we are now in our farming industry. We initially began by domesticating animals to aid us in growing our crops. Over the centuries, we have developed a technologically advanced process using automated high yield systems that are heavily dependent on GPS and sensors.

6. Functional efficiency will improve profitability

- **Cost efficiency to increase profits**
  You cannot expect a high valuation if you are only breaking even. Note that this is true apart from technological start-ups where valuation is based on future potential.

  Continuous improvement of products and business processes are essential to finding ways of increasing operational efficiency, cost reduction, and inventory controls without affecting operations.

- **Annual marketing plan**
  It is essential to adjust the marketing plan on a yearly basis to find ways to improve sales and market penetration, expansion into new markets and up-selling to current customers by offering new products and services. Focus on creating a diversified customer base that, ideally, generates recurring revenues.

Think about creating target market groups not only by considering a consumer's social and economic situations, but also their online and social media behavioral pattern. Currently, there are many algorithms to sort and refine data from search engines and social media. For example, Facebook and LinkedIn have different ways to identify and to narrow down target audience.

7. Create a winning culture

- **Recognize and reward**
  The people behind your company are the keys to your success. To make your company perform at optimum levels, you need to create a winning culture. To do this, the performance management needs to have a system with a strong emphasis on identifying the top performers

and ensuring that they were not only recognized but also well rewarded.

- **Working with the company rather than for the company**
  You need to create a strong feeling that you are working with everyone, rather than giving an impression that employees are working for the owners.

Finally, may I suggest some good practices for maintaining a solid valuation for your business? Please remember, your business is your hard work, both yours and your family's contributions and sacrifices. There are always many possible solutions for each scenario.

Making a conscious effort to maintain a valuation folder as part of your critical business and having a regular review and update working with your key team members, as well as external advisor teams, will only help you to derive maximum dollars for your business.

The most important thing I can advise you is to keep a positive attitude. There is never a dead end unless you decide it is a dead end. The world is filled with opportunities, and it is up to you to explore your options; there is no point in sulking on what cannot be changed. If you have done everything in your power and the results were not in your favor, do not take that as a failure, but rather a test of your strength and a learning center where you can only grow stronger for future opportunities.

About Rajasri

Rajasri Sriskandarajah has been serving for over 30 years helping companies become financialy healthy, wealthy and wise. His involvement has spanned manufacturing, distribution and service industries as Senior Executive, Advisor, and Leader, using his experience in accounting, financial management systems, best practices, and governance.

Driving business to get return on investment (ROI) requires education, diligence and confidence and entrepreneurial thinking, while continuing to review and address risks. And Raj has been able to deliver results and secure success for his clients and partners again and again. Raj has been a valuable asset for companies requiring not only advice related to strategies, smart goals, KPIs, and methods, but also operational matters such as management accounting, mergers and acquisitions, business development, business process improvement and tax advisories.

Using his years of experience, Raj has been heading his Accounting and Corporate Business Advisory practice under the brand name of "Rajasri CPA", as well as serving as a franchise partner of Padgett Business Services. Raj's work spans North America and Africa, serving in a variety of Senior Leadership roles to create successful ventures or lead expansions of businesses in revenues reaching millions of dollars in growth. To date, Raj is very active in providing his services to many Toronto-based companies who benefit from his expertise and experience.

An industry visionary, Raj is a business coach, strategist, and chartered professional accountant who builds financially-healthy enterprises, drives innovative solutions to business challenges and delivers streamlined accounting services. He maintains long-term relationships, develops sustainable solutions, and implements financial processes.

Raj attainted his MBA from the Richard Ivey School of Business, earned his ACMA and CGMA in Management Accounting from The Chartered Institute of Management Accountants, London, England, and admitted as a Certified General Accountant by CGA, Ontario, Canada. He also holds his membership with CPA - Chartered Professional Accountant of Ontario, Canada.

Raj is a family man with over 25 years of marriage to his partner Vasuki, and has two children who are continuing their higher education at universities. Raj is an active and contributing Community member serving a variety of communities in his neighborhood through his place of worship and via Rotary International service.

CHAPTER 4

REAL RELATIONSHIPS WITH YOUNG PEOPLE

BY DR. SABRINA WATSON

*There is nothing in a caterpillar that tells you it's going
to be a butterfly.*
~ R. Buckminster Fuller

Just as the caterpillar appears both unappealing at the beginning
of its life and a bit chaotic in its development, so too are the
early years of development for children and adolescents. Like
the caterpillar, there is not much in the current state of youth
development today that tells us what their true potential holds.
However, with the right support and empowerment from caring
adults, positive transformation can take shape, and the beauty
of seeing young people blossom will materialize like that of a
butterfly. Winning with young people takes relationships that
matter to young people. Imagine if most people thought of you as
being entitled, self-centered, lazy, and unmotivated. Imagine if,
as a young person, you go through your whole childhood feeling
the disapproval of most adults around you who name, claim and
blame many of society's problems on your generation. There
would not be much to celebrate.

Here is one example that can shed light on how we are doing, as
adults, relating to youth today. This is a speech given to parents

and teachers by a young high school student at a town-hall meeting concerning middle and high school students:

> *"You are proud of how you raised money for a new day-care center. You are proud that our football team made it to state this year. But in our daily lives, you no longer make time or take time. You don't know us, many of you are afraid of us, and when you pass by on the streets, you scurry by us. You don't know how to slow down and talk to us, and you are so much more fascinated by our problems than our success."*

Do we really know what's going on with young people today or are we missing opportunities to connect and win with them through positive developmental relationships? Although adults have valid concerns that cannot go unheard with what seems like a generation of young people who lack motivation, positive values, and possess too little respect for adults and commitment to hard work. These statements, however, only paint one side of the picture. Young people today by default of the time-period we live in, may not be responsible for what they have become in the eyes of society.

Consider for a moment the combination of factors that have influenced why young people may not be measuring up to most adults' expectations. What you will find is that young people did not get to this place on their own. There are multiple factors that have contributed to issues young people face—issues that may have played a hand in the current atmosphere among youth. It has been said that young people are the result of failed parenting, a failing education system, and being born in a technology-obsessed age where they are taught less about earning their rewards and everything about instant gratification. This has created a culture of young people with a love for things most adults consider useless (texting, chillin', and taking selfies to name a few), and a hatred for the qualities most adults consider worthy (hard work, reliability, and regard for authority).

The reality is that there is so much chaos in almost every aspect of young people's lives today—chaos in schools, families, peer groups and neighborhoods—there's no wonder why many of them so often drown-out the rest of the world with their social media and entertainment. Although most young people appear to have untouchable, arrogant, bigger-than-life attitudes, you'd be surprised to know that most young people have reported feeling alone, depressed, empty, and lost. Believe it or not—there is good news!

*Nothing—**nothing**—has more of an impact in the life of a young person than positive relationships.*
~ Dr. Peter Benson

This means that for all scenarios previously mentioned, there is hope and a pathway forward. It's all about relationships. This is where we can win with young people. It is the quality of close, caring relationships with caring adults—not just parents—who play an integral role in the support and development of youth. These adults include aunts, uncles, cousins, grandparents, coaches, mentors, teachers, neighbors, and leaders like me and you. A caring adult is a *difference maker*—someone who believes that all youth are capable of thriving if given the opportunity and the support needed for developing their strengths. Keep in mind that the best of human development, even for youth, happens from the inside-out and not from stuffing kids with facts and information in hopes that they will show success by passing tests or making good grades.

Leadership is at the heart of every sizable human achievement— even youth development. There is no better platform to have the conversation about positive youth than with leaders. Leaders are naturally people who want to add value to the lives of others. Leaders know what life is like when that inner spark is alive— the thing about life that brings you the greatest joy. How great it feels to wake up each morning to do what you love and to see others growing around you because of your influence. What if we shared this vision we have for ourselves with the young people around us? Each of us has the power to add this value to the life of a young person simply by helping them to identify that thing that gives their life direction, hope and purpose. Let us not take for granted that young people may or may not know what is special about them. We have to show them how to discover their inner spark that exists in each of themselves. A spark is a special quality, skill, or interest that makes a young person light up and that they are passionate about. Unfortunately, many youth have reported that no adult has ever asked them about their spark, therefore that spark remains dark and unused.

Many leaders and adults have already accepted that they have a role to play in caring for young people today. In this chapter, I hope to remind a few and persuade many others of the impact we could be making on an even greater scale, if we were more intentional about developing positive relationships, which I will share with you in this chapter. As leaders, the power lies with us to find new ways to leverage relationships with young people in our daily lives, even in our businesses and professional lives. This is where the change happens. According to the Search Institute, which has surveyed over five million children and adolescents internationally, there are five key areas in relationships that help young people thrive:

1. *Express care* – kids don't care what you know until they know that you care
2. *Challenge their growth* – kids need and often want to be stretched and challenged
3. *Provide support* – when you engage with kids you learn what goals that you can help them achieve
4. *Share power* – allow kids to have a voice and participate in the things that affect their lives
5. *Expand possibilities* – find opportunities where they can expand their minds and grow

Researchers found that when kids experience these five factors in relationships with caring adults, they have a greater chance of experiencing critical character strengths, such as motivation, perseverance, curiosity, and conscientiousness. My personal research has even indicated that this effect has a lasting impact that can produce wellness, social and emotional competence into adulthood.

I have been trained as a facilitator by Search Institute on Developmental Assets, helping adults find ways to develop relationships that matter to youth, and I train youth on developing the leader within. Additionally, my personal research has put the focus on relationships with youth from struggling families, single parent families, families of divorce, and LGBTQ families. I wanted to know if kids facing numerous hardships in school and at home would benefit similarly from these kinds of positive relationships. After five years of researching these matters, the answer is 'yes'. Even youth living in difficult environments show that positive relationships can have a positive effect on their developmental track. *A young person who is struggling to thrive can be guided and redirected towards developing in a positive, healthy direction through the power of a positive relationship with a caring adult.*

What would actually happen if we focused on the strengths of young people rather than their deficits? The answer is, they would thrive! When young people thrive, school success increases, school engagement increases, compassion increases, sense of purpose increases, and the list goes on. We have viewed young people for so long through a deficit lens focusing on what they lack and the problems they create rather than focusing on the strengths they possess.

This deficit perspective has guided even research and public policy, costing the United States hundreds of millions of dollars each year for research based just on understanding the problems of youth. With more than 80 million youth in this country between the ages of 0 and 18, this is a problem that affects us all—and it's growing. If we don't change the way we view young people and if we don't start acknowledging the gifts and talents these young people bring to our world, then the price we neglect to pay today with real relationships will be the greatest threat to our economy and our society tomorrow.

Take a look at what young people really think and feel; it will reveal some unexpected results and possibly open doors towards real hope and solutions. A survey conducted by the Search Institute found that 80% of youth between the ages of 12 and 25 expressed the following life goals as being very important to them:

- *Being hopeful about the future*
- *Having a sense that life has meaning and purpose*
- *Making the world a better place*
- *Protecting the earth's air, land, and water*
- *Knowing what is unique and valuable about themselves*

These are not the results you would expect from the young people we've been discussing. How can young people truly feel this way internally while their actions reflect so contrary to this effect externally? It's an indication that something is missing. When adults become more engaged with young people on a personal level, we will find that many of them express their desire for joy and purpose in their lives, and isn't this what adults actually want to see? Caring adults are needed to show young people how to form deep and meaningful relationships. The real MVPs (Most Valuable People) in the lives of youth today are the ones willing to show-up as caring adults for a young person using the five keys to successful relationships. I believe leaders who know how to effect change are the greatest champions for this cause, leaders who are willing to help young people come out of the darkness of oblivion and into the light of awareness. Those who are willing to invest in young people today will have the greatest impact on our world tomorrow.

Leadership is influence and influence can be the difference maker in the life of young people.

EXAMPLES OF WHAT YOU CAN DO TO WIN WITH YOUTH, TO HELP THEM THRIVE AND BECOME THEIR BEST SELVES:

As a Caring Adult:	You can impact youth around you by:	Which will build assets in youth and...
An educator or teacher	Asking students for their help in solving classroom disputes or problems. Discover students' interests and gifts outside of school. Find ways to integrate their passion with upcoming assignments. Let students know you believe in them and won't give up on them – communicate this verbally in a one-on-one setting.	Create a positive learning environment where youth feel connected and have a sense of belonging – no matter where they come from.
A Non-parental, caring adult	Start a neighborhood watch for the youth in your community. Do small things like addressing youth by their names.	The more supervision, monitoring, and support from caring adults, the better the outcome, even in the long term for youth.
Parents can launch a teen into adulthood	By encouraging their self-awareness and self-knowledge by offering suggestions but allowing them to make their own choices based on their own needs. Offer a listening ear that does not judge, even if you disagree, and an anchor that provides perspective about the changes they're going through.	Produce social and emotional competence at an age when they need them most.

THE POWER OF LEADERS TO RESHAPE OUR FUTURE WITH YOUTH

Real Relationships with Young People is the perfect platform for mentors, leaders and coaches who know exactly how to plug-in, get-connected, and how to leverage relationships.

One of the best ways to discover what you have to offer young people is to think back to your own childhood experiences. Who was that someone in your life who encouraged you, who supported your ideas, who believed in you? Chances are, because of those difference makers in your life, you and many others have become invaluable members of society today. The stats below show the real impact that positive relationships with youth could have on our economy:

Take a look at these taken from John Maxwell's book, *Talent is Never Enough:*

- More than 50% of all CEOs of Fortune 500 companies had C or C- averages in college.
- 65% of all US Senators came from the bottom half of their school classes.
- 75% of US Presidents were in the lower half club in school.
- More than 50% of millionaire entrepreneurs never finished college.

As we see here, some of our beliefs around what young people are lacking need to be re-examined and we need to begin to see them for their gifts and talents they offer to the world. How can each of us be a difference maker? How can we nurture the gifts and talents of a young person we may have not even noticed before? This is how we transform this generation and produce the next generation of successful CEOs, senators, presidents, and millionaires.

If you have ever thought that young people are hopeless and going nowhere, consider this fact: according to developmental scientist Dr. Peter Benson, "… **nothing—*nothing* – has more of an impact in the life of a young person than positive relationships**." Each of us has our own desires to make a difference in the life of a young person. Change is possible with simple efforts of engagement of youth, even if only for one youth. We will then begin to see the change we want to see in young people. Each of us has our own gifts, talents, and strengths as leaders and this is where you can begin to transform the lives of young people in your circles by helping them to find their own gifts, talents and strengths.

The bottom line is that when we win with young people, we win for us all.

About Dr. Sabrina

Dr. Sabrina Watson is a Positive Youth Development Strategist and Speaker who partners with educators, CEOs, Millennials, youth leaders and parents activating developmental relationships in Schools, Churches, and Community Organizations. Her work with youth in these groups helps to boost motivation and achievement for youth and produce positive outcomes for the organizations. Dr. Sabrina is the CEO of LEADA, LLC, an organization that provides consulting, training and workshops supporting schools, churches, and organizations looking to increase youth performance in classrooms, homes, on the job and in life.

After spending more than a decade working as a classroom teacher in public education and raising two children as a single mother (after the untimely death of their father), Dr. Sabrina knows what truly drives young people to succeed in the classroom and in life. She understands how to connect with the heart-beat of today's youth that many organizations are trying to accomplish. Dr. Sabrina spent eight years researching strategies that promote positive social and emotional outcomes in youth. She has been trained on Developmental Relationships by Search Institute, the leading authority in research on practices that help young people become their best selves. Dr. Sabrina is also Kolbe Systems™ Certified in providing strategies for improving individual and group performance.

Dr. Sabrina is a Best-Selling Author of the book, *What It Takes To Win*, with co-author Brian Tracy. She is also the author of the Pinnacle Award-winning book, *When You Have to be The Man* – a book for single mothers revealing the power of parenting as Christian women. In addition to her extensive knowledge and expertise on topics relating to parenting and positive youth development, she is a founding partner of the John Maxwell Certified Leadership Coaches and Speakers. Dr. Sabrina is a dynamic speaker, one who knows how to connect with her audience. Dr. Sabrina holds a B.S. in psychology, an MA in Early Childhood Development, and a Ph.D. in Family Studies and Intervention Strategies.

Dr. Sabrina will be hosting a National Event in the Fall of 2019 for youth "The Future You Event" in Orlando, Florida (www.futureyou.biz).

CHAPTER 5

THE STATE OF YOUR SEO: TAKE A MINUTE AND TAKE STOCK

BY LINDSAY DICKS

Sometimes, when our website is humming along, seemingly doing everything it's meant and supposed to do, we fall into the "set-it-and-forget-it" mindset. In other words, we figure, "If it ain't broke, don't fix it."

Until it is. Broken, that is. Suddenly, something goes wrong. Maybe pages that looked great don't display right? Perhaps you stop getting contact form completions? Or distressingly, you are no longer ranking in Google for terms you used to dominate?

In any case, for some reason or other, it quickly becomes clear— you should have been paying more attention to your website all along.

The moral of the story should be clear...

Don't ever get complacent with the state of your site. The risks are too great. Wise 'webionados' do this. Don't you want to be a wise webionado too?

Let's talk about how to join that group—the smart website owners who frequently take stock of their website, its effectiveness and efficiency as well as its visibility. And, who also course correct when they expect it might be needed soon, but before it really becomes an emergency.

I.   Website Design Review

Some website design trends can change on a dime. Web design best practices, however, stay pretty constant.

In general, if you want or need to get by with making design tweaks and alterations as seldom as possible, keeping it simple is usually the best option. Clean, minimal-special-effect and not-overly-designed sites carry many benefits. It's easy to sometimes think we need a lot of cool features, brilliant copy and a ton of text to have a "great" website. Yet, in most cases, less is truly 'more.'

One good thing about a minimalistic website design is that it forces you to really dial in to what you want – and need – to say, to attract and convert leads. It gets right to the point, maximizing and respecting your prospects' precious time (an average time on site for STRONG websites is 2 minutes!).

Another is that there is less that can 'go wrong' with design. If you focus on crisp visuals and value-driven content, you rarely go wrong.

According to Website Magazine[1] -- here are what their experts consider the five biggest benefits of simple websites:

1. Simple websites convert better.
2. Simple web designs load faster.
3. Simple designs are more mobile-friendly.
4. Simple websites cost less.
5. Simple websites reduce user friction.

1. https://www.websitemagazine.com/blog/the-undeniable-benefits-of-simple-website-design

II.   Conversion Testing and Optimization

When it comes to conversion, what 'works' stays fairly constant, but there is almost always room for improvement.

As with most things, the conversion ratios you experience in the beginning—or when you first start working on the conversion process—seem fantastic! Then, over time, you yearn for 'more' and 'better.' When you start to feel that way, be sure not to throw the baby out with the bath water. In other words, don't just assume that something is 'wrong' and you need to trash everything and start over.

Instead, you should consider what you can test and improve to make your conversion numbers better. Some of the things to test – usually utilizing a specific type of web conversion analysis and optimization called "A/B Testing." This is where you will test one change against a constant. Another is called "multivariate testing" – where you will test multiple elements of your conversion process.

Here are some factors of your website you might consider examining and where you might try to improve conversion:

- Landing page or page / post titles
- Landing page or page / post headlines and sub-headlines
- Colors (of titles, headlines and other elements)
- Fonts
- Copy
- Calls-to-action
- The text on submission buttons
- Fields you are requesting be completed on forms
- Where forms are positioned on a page
- Upsells, cross-sells and one-time offers

III.   SEO: Performing a Website Audit

Don't wait for your rank to take a tumble—or start to decline—before checking the state of your search engine optimization. There are many tools out there that can help you perform a thorough website SEO audit and they make it quick, easy and painless.

The tools to assist you in performing a full and comprehensive website audit can, however, be a little pricey. Thus, you might want to check and see if your website provider, web designer or SEO firm offers such a service. This also gives you the added benefit of usually having someone there who can help you fix or correct any issues that might be found.

Here are some things a good website SEO audit will take a look at:

- If your URLS are "clean"
- Whether there is a Robots.txt file present and configured correctly
- If your site has an XML site map and it's been submitted to the search engines
- That the site does not use flash or frames
- If meta titles and descriptions are present and not duplicated
- If heading tags are present and utilized properly
- If the site is Open Auth compliant
- If structured data and schema are present and correctly identified
- If the site is AMP ready
- If knowledge graph data is present and written right
- Whether all images have correct titles and alt tags
- The status of internal and outbound links, as well as the links coming in to the site (inbound links)
- Whether inbound and external links have optimized anchor text
- That content is keyword rich but not overly spammy

- Server response time
- The presence and importance of any 404 (page not found) errors
- Whether code is clean and minimized where possible
- If the site passes W3C HTML validation

While you obviously can't predict or foresee everything that might go wrong with your website, the ideas and tips above should at least help you be protected and prepared. Ultimately, that's the best you can do – for yourself and for the health of your business. For those whose business depends on website health, this is especially critical. And it's really too simple to not address up-front, in advance.

About Lindsay

Lindsay Dicks helps her clients tell their stories in the online world. Being brought up around a family of marketers, but a product of Generation Y, Lindsay naturally gravitated to the new world of on-line marketing. Lindsay began freelance writing in 2000 and soon after launched her own PR firm that thrived by offering an in-your-face "Guaranteed PR" that was one of the first of its type in the nation.

Lindsay's new media career is centered on her philosophy that "people buy people." Her goal is to help her clients build a relationship with their prospects and customers. Once that relationship is built and they learn to trust them as the expert in their field, then they will do business with them. Lindsay also built a proprietary process that utilizes social media marketing, content marketing and search engine optimization to create online "buzz" for her clients that helps them to convey their business and personal story. Lindsay's clientele spans the entire business map and ranges from doctors and small business owners to Inc. 500 CEOs.

Lindsay is a graduate of the University of Florida. She is the CEO of CelebritySites™, an online marketing company specializing in social media and online personal branding. Lindsay is recognized as one of the top online marketing experts in the world and has co-authored more than 25 bestselling books alongside authors such as Steve Forbes, Richard Branson, Brian Tracy, Jack Canfield (creator of the *Chicken Soup for the Soul* series), Dan Kennedy, Robert Allen, Dr. Ivan Misner (founder of BNI), Jay Conrad Levinson (author of the *Guerilla Marketing* series), Leigh Steinberg and many others, including the breakthrough hit *Celebrity Branding You!*

She has also been selected as one of America's PremierExperts™ and has been quoted in *Forbes, Newsweek, The Wall Street Journal, USA Today,* and *Inc.* magazine as well as featured on NBC, ABC, and CBS television affiliates – speaking on social media, search engine optimization and making more money online. Lindsay was also brought on FOX 35 News as their Online Marketing Expert.

Lindsay, a national speaker, has shared the stage with some of the top speakers in the world, including Brian Tracy, Lee Milteer, Ron LeGrand,

Arielle Ford, Leigh Steinberg, Dr. Nido Qubein, Dan Sullivan, David Bullock, Peter Shankman and many others. Lindsay was also a Producer on the Emmy-winning film, *Jacob's Turn*, and sits on the advisory board for the Global Economic Initiative.

You can connect with Lindsay at:
- Lindsay@CelebritySites.com
- www.twitter.com/LindsayMDicks
- www.facebook.com/LindsayDicks

CHAPTER 6

VICTORY TOWER

BY STACY BRYANT

Failure will never overtake me if my will to win is strong enough.
~ Coach Stacy

[*will* (wil) n. The mental faculty by which one deliberately chooses or decides upon a course of action.]

The question often lingers in my head, why are so many people unsuccessful? What is it that keeps people from reaching their full potential? What is it that keeps one from living out their dreams? What is it that keeps one from living their best life?

After working with people over the years in personal development, I find that the one thing missing that keeps people stuck with the mentality of unsuccess, is the very will to win.

The will to win can make or break you. Yes, there are many other characteristics that play into success, but without the will to win, none of the others matter.

Like many people, my life story is not one of many great achievements, or a loving functional upbringing. There are many experiences that I have come across in life that are experiences that can break a person's will. Experiences that will crush you to the core. Experiences that will absolutely make you want to throw in the towel. But through it all, somehow, I found the will to win.

I joined the army later in life than the average soldier. Over 30, ready to start life anew, and a slight will to win. When I joined, I had just severed a brutal domestic violent relationship with my now ex-husband. I was running from him, not sure where else to turn, or how to begin to pick up the pieces to my disheveled non-functioning life. At the time, I had three children and did not have a clue what was next. I was determined to rise, but I really didn't know how. So, I took a chance, with the little bit of will I had left, and joined the army. And it was not an easy task. As a middle-aged woman joining a highly-structured physical organization, it was not effortless.

The second phase of basic training consisted of a field training exercise, a foot march, marksmanship training, and the infamous confidence course. I am afraid of heights, so the confidence course was devastating.

The confidence course consists of several obstacle courses in one. For the most part, all the courses were fun and challenging. The last course is called the Slide for Life. You climb up a 10 ft pole tower and then lower yourself down at a drop. Being afraid of heights sent me into a frenzy. I contemplated it in my head repeatedly. And I was extremely terrified. My drill sergeant assured me that I would be ok, but that did not stop the butterflies. Standing there looking at how high off the ground I had to climb, I had second thoughts of whether this was the right career for me. To someone afraid of heights, 10 feet looks like 100 feet.

A fellow soldier walks up to me and says, "Wow! You have fear written all over your face. I cannot believe you are going to let these fresh-out-of-high school kids show you up." Now, my first thought was, I really don't care. There is no way I'm going to climb that high off the ground and ride some rope down with nothing to catch me if I fall. There was something to catch me, but it didn't look safe enough to me. I now know that was fear talking to me in my head, but I would not have passed the phase if I didn't do it. After standing there watching another ten people go through the line, I paced for several more moments and mustered up all the will I had within myself and did it. It felt good to conquer that fear. Little did I know there was more in store for me.

To complete basic training, you must complete every phase. Within every phase you must complete each obstacle or test. Going to the last and final phase was victory. And I do mean that literally. The last and final obstacle was completing Victory Tower. I believe they do it now in the first phase, but in my class, it was last. They didn't talk about it much and there is a reason for that. It is definitely something that you have to muster up all your will, prayers, blessings, or whatever you can grab a hold of, to help get you through it.

As I was presented with Victory Tower, I fainted. When the drill sergeant announced that it was 40 ft, I got so dizzy and nauseated, I almost fainted again. Victory Tower is another type of confidence course where you must climb 40 feet and propel down a rope. Almost the same as before, but a little different . . . and higher.

As I recovered from my fainting spell, I immediately decided that this was not for me. There is no way I was climbing up that wall. At that moment going back to a life of uncertainty, doom, and abuse seemed much better. But only for an inkling.

The pacing began again. I started to weigh my options. I quickly calculated my pros and cons. I thought about my life before the day I arrived at basic training. Abusive husband, barely making it, one dead-end job after another. Is that really what I wanted to go back too? All I could think about is how disgusted I was with contemplating going back to an unstable household. Before I could think anymore, I was climbing up the wall. I did not even think about it until I got to the top. Once I got to the top, I wanted to faint again. All I could hear was, "good job private." I am still thinking why in the world are they saying good job? Don't they know I have to get down? What is such a good job about climbing up a 40-foot wall 'scared crapless.'

Standing at the top, I'm thinking, basic training changes the trajectory of my life for the positive and better. Where did I get the will to even get up the wall? Now I must muster the will to get down. No more not knowing where the next meal was coming from. No more homeless shelters. No more shifting here to there, not feeling like a good mother. No more! The will to win comes out of nowhere when you are ready.

At that moment the propel latch snapped and the drill sergeant said, "Alright private, 40 rounds." Which meant, you're connected, your turn. I dried my tears and turned around and dropped.

I DID IT! I'M STILL ALIVE! I made it to the bottom and I am still alive! I did it. One of the biggest challenges I have ever had to face, and I did it. I was shaking in my boots the entire time. Literally.

What really got me over that wall was the WILL TO WIN. Not wanting to go back to a dysfunctional life . . . wanting to be a better provider for my children . . . wanting more for my life. The will to do that got me over that wall. And from that moment on, I began a cycle of winning.

WHAT IT TAKES TO WIN

1. Made Up Mind

I have concluded that to instill 'the will to win' into your subconscious you have to first and foremost have a made-up mind. See, when I found myself at the top of Victory Tower I realized that at that moment my mind was made up.

My mind was made up to move forward and be successful in life. It was made up that I would not be turning back and settling anymore. I would not go back and continue to teach my children 'stinking' thinking. I had completely and utterly decided to propel down that wall and walk into a new life. There is nothing more powerful than a made-up mind. You really must take into consideration, every day of your life, what condition or state of mind your mind is in.

Have you noticed that you have different reactions for all the many different situations that arise? There are many times when I have been able to quickly solve an issue, and there are many times when it has taken me so much time to come up with a solution that I end up filled with all sorts of self-doubt. When your mind is undisciplined you are insecure, anxious and uncertain. You no longer have the tenacity or the will to WIN. When you develop determination to do or be something, your life changes dramatically. As an army veteran, the will to win was instilled in my training. The object is to win … to beat the opponent … to not bend to distractions … to remain focused on the mission …. to dwell in the positive outcome.

2. Commitment

After your mind is made up, you must focus on the commitment. Yes, your mind can be totally made up and you will, at that point, talk yourself out of it. How important is it for you, and what are you willing to sacrifice to achieve it? If you find yourself fully committed, motivation will follow. All people set goals and then easily slip back into old habits. We are all haunted by excuses that have cost us countless opportunities for growth. So many people are attached to comfort and safety. To truly grow and expand we must find an area of our life where commitment supersedes comfort.

Regardless of the lemons that life decided to throw at me,

once my mind was made up, I focused on the commitment using three keys. These are:

- sacrifice
- purpose
- determination

I sacrificed my fear and climbed that wall. I knew there was a bigger purpose and held on to it. And I made it down that wall because I was determined.

3. Guard your thoughts

Your thoughts will influence your feelings. Your feelings then determine how you view things. As I was contemplating climbing that tower, thoughts were racing through my mind. Of course, the negative thoughts were kicking in. But what made me climb that wall was focusing on the thoughts that moved me forward and not the thoughts I had filled with fears. You have a lot of thoughts in your head, and you always have a choice of which ones to focus on, the ones that will make you emotionally stuck (fears) or the ones that will move you forward (stepping out of your comfort zone).

4. Think Big

When you think BIG, your will bends to your BIG thinking. Imagine if Denzel Washington had not thought big when that lady in the beauty parlor spoke into his life on that day in 1975. The lady in the beauty parlor that day told him that he was going to travel the world and speak to millions of people. He said he had not really planned anything outside of joining the military because he was failing college. But at that moment, he learned a very important lesson, and from that point on, he thought big. He is now one of the number one actors in the world. When you think big, your will bends to your big thinking.

The *will to win* leaves no room for compromise. There is not a lot of room for quitting when you have the will to win. Like many people, my beginning was not pretty. Molestation, sexual assault, teen dysfunction, multiple suicide attempts, major depression, mental health issues, domestic violence survivor, cancer survivor, and working 'to get by' to raise five kids alone. The bowl of cherries missed me. Many people would have given up a very long time ago.

But that day I climbed Victory Tower, I changed it all. I wiped away all excuses and distractions. There was no longer any room to compromise. I walked away with what it takes to win, the will to win!

About Stacy

Stacy Bryant, also known as (Coach Stacy), is the founder of The Stiletto Bosses Network™ and The Free Hope Foundation for Domestic Violence. She is the host of *Candid Conversation with Coach Stacy* on 108 Praise Radio in Atlanta Georgia. Coach Stacy is also the CEO of ICU Coaching Academy, where she trains and certifies Life Coaches with a passion. She is a Retired Veteran of the United States Army and she devotes her life to empowering others. Her goal is to assist and empower people all over the world by instilling and expressing confidence in themselves. Her focus is to empower people by helping them with their finances, relationships, entrepreneurship, health, faith, and life.

Stacy is a Certified Master Life Coach Trainer, Author, Speaker, and Radio Personality. Her passion for inspiring and encouraging others has made her a sought-after Inspirational Speaker and Coach. She is the author of *Building Self-Confidence* and the *Her Story* series. Coach Stacy has a bachelor's degree in Business Administration and is currently pursuing her MBA.

Stacy has walked the road of a survivor her entire life and is passionate about personal development. She is dedicated to helping others rise above their circumstances. Her mission in life is to encourage and empower others to explore and find out who they are –inside and out. From there, she believes they will be able to create the life they have always dreamed of.

You can connect with Stacy at:
- Stacy@stacybryant.com
- www.facebook.com/TheCoachStacy/
- www.twitter.com/coachstacy2222

CHAPTER 7

CHANGE YOUR WORDS AND CHANGE YOUR WORLD

BY TERRI MATTHEWS

By the young age of 18 years old, I was the single mother of one of the most beautiful human beings I've ever met. I didn't have a lot of parental support during that time because my parents were battling their own demons, so I learned early on how to fend for myself. Life stacked some pretty unfair obstacles against me with molestation, homelessness, abuse… you name it.

I have personally witnessed people facing my same set of obstacles either cave or conquer. Thanks be to God, it was the latter for me… in the midst of all of the turmoil of my life, I learned resiliency from my grandfather. His distant lessons showed me that I was strong enough to withstand whatever came my way. Because of those lessons, I adopted an *I Can* mentality at around 10 or 11 years of age. It started with real simplistic words like, 'I can handle this' or 'I can overcome that.' In my eyes, life forced me to become my own superhero. The "S" I wore on my chest was the scripture, Romans 8:28 (KJV), *"I can do all things through Christ who strengthens me."*

I went on to tackle life, becoming a successful businesswoman, mother and wife. But still, in my life of *I Cans*, I felt this internal longing to go further and to do more. So, I began to write out a long list of all the things I envisioned and that God showed me. I was very excited about writing out the vision because that meant I tackled the first part of the process as instructed in Habakkuk 2:2 (KJV), "Write the vision, and make it plain upon tables."

When I periodically went back to read the items on that list, I noticed that the completion box next to many of the items was left unchecked. It wasn't that I didn't have the ability to complete what was on the list, as I knew I could do them, but why wasn't I? I suppose it was life or excuses that got in the way of completion, I don't know... After many months and years went by, I grew tired and frustrated with my incomplete list and that's when God really got my attention and forced me to make a monumental shift that wrecked my world completely. It was in those moments of frustration I understood that God's vision for my life superseded what I could do on my own strength, knowledge and ability.

God began to challenge everything I knew about myself. I discovered two very important things about myself and the I Can mentality. The first thing was that *I Can* didn't demand any follow through. It was simply a proclamation of one's own ability. And secondly, as much as I thought I was leaning and depending on God, *I Can* didn't require me to trust God at all. I realized that I reduced God to what I could accomplish with my own resources and capacity. I had no faith outside of what I could make happen on my own. If I was going to accomplish the things that God showed me and that I wrote down on that list, I would have to shift the narrative on both levels.

First, I had to change my language from *I Can* to *I will*. *I will* is not just a proclamation of ability, it is much more than that. *I will* became the directive that propelled me into action. This simple, yet incredibly powerful change in words, challenged me and forced me to be accountable because it signified a supporting action immediately followed my declaration.

Often, there are things God is calling us to do and because we've been taught scriptures like Philippians 4:13 (KJV), *"I can do all things through Christ who strengthens me,"* we acknowledge that in God we can do incredible things. But the real questions are, will we and do we even trust God at all?

After that adjustment, I had to shift *I will* to *I WILL*, which later became my response to God when He challenged me to grow up in my faith and to accept and execute His vision for my life on His terms. God knows I can write a check and I have and will write plenty more of them. But when God says, "sell everything you have because I have a different plan for your life" or "take your children and move to a place where you don't know anybody," will your response to God be: *I WILL?* It was not easy for me to comply to those requests from God, but eventually I surrendered my will to His WILL and have been blessed exponentially because of my obedience.

The question I have for you reading this is, will you? Will you heal? Will you pray? Will you answer the call?

Understand, God created us all with a purpose. He has a call on every one of our lives. He's allowed certain situations to arise that challenge us and grow us and He's given us the Holy Spirit to have the ability to do all things, if we *WILL*. Whenever you feel weakened or defeated, it's important you understand that you are not alone in taking action. The Holy Spirit is your partner in execution because it's not possible to do an *I WILL* without God.

If you're not journaling, I challenge you to start. If you are, I challenge you to be transparent in it. Let God speak to your heart as you are writing. This may seem new and unfamiliar especially in business, but it's a fairly simple process and you start by just being honest with yourself. Be transparent about what you think and feel. God doesn't want us to remain the same. We are walking billboards for Him and all of us have different experiences that collectively come together for our greater purpose.

Think of journaling as a way to start looking at real life places where you can actually make a change. Begin with the foundational stuff so you can build something that withstands the test of time and trials.

Sometimes, when people want to heal, they can't, because they aren't being honest with themselves. Nobody wants to admit they're still hurting because of an "ex" or they're still dealing with bitterness from childhood trauma and rejection. Everybody wants to look good on the outside like they have it all together, but that's just not true for everyone. We all have fears. We all struggle. Your kids really do get on your nerves. Whatever *it* is, it's about being honest with yourself and honesty requires doing some digging, and that digging has to be done in a safe space.

When being transparent in writing, this is where you start to repair your broken places. It doesn't mean you have to stop everything you're doing. It just means that you have to make sure your foundation is level. One of the businesses I own is a construction company. When building, if the dirt isn't right, you've got a problem. You can't even pour concrete unless the ground is excavated. Excavating is how you create a level ground to make sure what you're going to build won't sink. Your personal excavation process is God teaching us not to build our lives on sinking sand. Understand that you are the foundation of your life and every business or relationship you establish. You have to be excavated. You have got to be cleaned out.

Think about anytime someone builds a house. The longest period is spent on the foundation. Once the foundation is right, the walls go up in 30 days or so. Everything moves quickly once the foundation is laid. Until then, you'll be looking at the ground and wondering when they're going to start working. Sometimes, it looks like they're just shoveling and moving dirt around and then you start to question the process.

Even though you can't see the finished work, understand that through every phase of this process God is moving things around for your good. The fear that most people have is of time. "If I take the time to work on me or if I take the time to do all these things, it's going to take me so much longer to execute my dream."

But, if you go ahead and build anything, without the ground being on solid foundation, it will crack, it will lean and it will crumble under pressure. You are digging to find out more about you, so you can lay your sure foundation. Saying, *I will* and *I WILL*, is a part of your excavation process. It allows you to remove damaged things from your life so you can pour only what's necessary into your foundation.

During this process you will come across some rocky areas in your past, places where you just buried the hurt and kept going. There will be obstacles, but that does not give you the green light to stop digging. It means you must acknowledge these are the cracks or concerns that could ruin your foundation.

If you don't get your thoughts, your heart, your mind around what those things are, sure you can go ahead and build, but somewhere within your building, what you didn't excavate and what you didn't deal with shoveling, moving out or acknowledging, will manifest itself somewhere else in what you're building.

Saying *I WILL* is like pouring the right substances into your foundation. It's acknowledging that you don't have to build your life out of brokenness. You don't have to build your life out of pain and don't have to build your life out of shame. Use your *I WILLS* to help build your foundation. Set them as the building blocks for your life's vision. Write them down as instructed by God in Habakkuk 2:2.

Journaling will take you on a journey of self-discovery. I must warn you that this process will only work if you do. It will challenge you to be authentic, transparent, honest and accountable, so that you can rise to the best version of yourself. You must have the courage to dig within yourself, be accountable to yourself and be willing to listen to yourself in order to get the results intended.

I challenge you to use it as a reminder to focus less on the problems and more on the promises. Use *I WILL* to increase your faith, strengthen your heart, and walk in your purpose. Use it to encourage yourself and become your own cheerleader, warrior and doer. The last question I have for you is, **WILL you do it?**

About Terri

There is not a single word that could describe Terri Matthews and culminate the essence of her purpose and mission.

"Is she a Trailblazer?"

"Is she an Innovator?"

"Is she considered the Olivia Pope of business?"

Those who are in the know, would concur!

Terri Matthews is a faith-made serial entrepreneur, motivational speaker, Autism Advocate and TV host of an AU-Some show called, *On the Spectrum*, which covers All Things Autism!

As a businesswoman, Terri has established thriving organizations in the following industries: clothing, construction, healthcare, environmental, technology and consulting. She prides herself in building brands rooted in consciousness, community and empowerment.

Beyond success in the corporate and entrepreneurial space, Terri's passion is ignited most when helping others overcome obstacles in life and achieving their dreams. She motivates and educates from experience, using her own background and early challenges to bridge the gap between struggle and success with her Next Level Vision Series Platform. She has delivered keynotes to audiences from 300 to over 30,000 globally through panels, faith-based conferences, seminars, educational organizations, corporate gatherings and much more.

Terri's greatest inspiration comes from her children. Her son, Jaden, now 11 years old was diagnosed with autism at the age of three. She dedicated tremendous amounts of time and money to ensure Jaden received the most advanced therapies available, and founded Jaden's Voice, Inc. in 2010 to advocate and provide options to those with limited resources.

To further her mission on autism awareness, Terri launched her new show, *On the Spectrum*, www.onthespectrum.tv, where she marries her congenial personality, entrepreneurial acumen and autism advocacy experience to offer support and share light on autism. *On the Spectrum* is a fun and exciting show offering a refreshing perspective on autism to help the world navigate the spectrum of autism. She likes to call it: "Prescription TV!"

If you walked a mile in Terri's shoes, her journey would leave these words of reflection:

"Coming from modest beginnings, I am certainly no stranger to adversity; yet, I am a firm believer that God shines through the cracks of broken people to illuminate hope and light for the world. So never give up on yourself... There is purpose in your pain."

CHAPTER 8

WHAT IT TAKES TO WIN IN EMAIL MARKETING

BY KOKCHIN CHOW

EMAIL MARKETING

When you sign up to receive email newsletters from your favorite blog or email updates from your favorite store, you're giving that person or business permission to send you emails. And it's the email sender's responsibility to give you what you signed up for; whether it's an email newsletter or a limited time sale.

As you receive those emails, you might notice that you grow more attached to the brand, engage with their content and maybe buy a product or two. When all of that happens – relationship building, customer nurturing and business growing – that's email marketing.

Please note it's not about sending spammy messages or buying email lists. And it's more than simply sending commercial emails to others. Email marketing is about making real connections with people who want to hear from you. It's about communicating with multiple people at one time (in a way that feels like a 1:1 conversation), building relationships and growing your brand as a result.

GROW YOUR BUSINESS WITH EMAIL

For many small business owners, bloggers and entrepreneurs, managing the daily operations of a brand is a full-time, borderline 24/7 job. While you may try playing a jack-of-all-trades, you have probably encountered a few (or many) times where it's felt like there's never enough time to do it all.

Juggling all those responsibilities often can cause certain things to fall to the wayside, like marketing or building an audience. You're already struggling with managing the "essential" tasks, how could you possibly add another thing to your to do list.

With email marketing however, promoting your business and connecting with your audience becomes a whole lot easier – and that's only a snapshot of the bigger email marketing picture. Now, you may have heard that email was declared "dead" just a few years ago. With the rise of social media, many assumed it had become irrelevant – and therefore ready to join the final resting place of 'has-been' marketing tactics like phone books and telemarketing.

But we were proved wrong. As creating educational content to engage and build relationships with customers became the cornerstone for every blogger and business, email evolved with it. Today, email marketing is one of the most effective ways to not only communicate with an audience, but to build your brand as well.

Just look at the benefits:

Email marketing delivers a return of 4,300 percent! Plus, it's more cost-effective than other forms of marketing. And it frees up your time, so you can get back to running your business.
Best of all, consumers love it!

The stats don't lie:

- Almost a third of consumers prefer to receive communication from brands via email.
- 66 percent of consumers have made a purchase online as a result of an email marketing message.
- 138 percent more is spent by consumers who receive email offers than those who don't.

Aside from the opportunities to grow your business, email marketing also can help build a community of loyal customers.

Imagine this scenario for a moment:

A bright-eyed individual is exploring your website. She looks around a few pages, but leaves with an empty shopping cart when she doesn't see a sweater in her favorite color. Maybe she'll return and consider making a purchase, but the chances are slim.

Now, imagine if there was a way for her to hear from you again; a chance to sign up on your email list and guarantee future interactions. These might lead to a satisfied customer who found a sweater in the perfect shade of teal.

Email becomes so much more than just another way to advertise your brand. It's a way to make real connections with those who are truly interested in your business.

Considering that most people prefer to communicate with brands through the inbox, email marketing is a no-brainer.

PLAN AN EMAIL STRATEGY

Before you can begin collecting email subscribers or importing them into your list, you should first take some time to think about your email marketing strategy – which starts with identifying your expectations and goals.

Set Goals

As you think about what you hope to achieve through email marketing, it will be helpful to ask yourself:

- How do you want your emails to help your business?
- Do you want to increase sales for your product?
- Do you want to build relationships with subscribers?
- Who is the ideal subscriber for your email list?
- How will it fit in with your overall marketing strategy?

While these goals may change or evolve over time, it's important to consider the purpose of your emails and to set goals that are both measurable and attainable.

For those just starting out with email marketing, you might want to focus your goal on growing subscribers.

In this case, your goal might look like the following: I plan to collect 500 email subscribers over the next 12 months by leveraging online and offline opportunities to attract sign ups.

By including a numeric value, a due date and a general idea of how you plan on meeting that number, you will have a clear target to work towards. It can even provide guidance for executing tactics that'll help you achieve your end goal.

As you plan your tactics, also consider the target audience you hope to reach. For example, a fitness trainer with a focus on health and wellness might target people who are just getting started with exercising and changing their diet.

Understanding your ideal customers will help you determine the best ways to connect and communicate with them.

GROW YOUR EMAIL LIST

An engaged list of subscribers is the key to email marketing success. But it's not just about how many subscribers you have, it's about having the right people who are interested in your brand and what you have to with share with them.

To help you grow your list and attract a quality email subscriber, there are a few steps you need to follow. And it all begins with the sign-up form.

Create A Sign-Up Form:
The sign-up form is where your website visitors submit their email address in order to subscribe to your list and get your emails. These forms can also allow you to obtain other information, like name, geographical location, specific interests and more.

The Copy:
Your form should tell your readers exactly what they are going to get after signing up to your list. Will you be sending them a weekly newsletter? ... Product promotions? Setting clear expectations will be key to attracting quality subscribers who want to hear from you ... and staying out of the spam folder.

The Call-to-Action:
This is the part of your sign-up form where you ask readers to take a specific action. In this case, your call-to-action (CTA) is to sign up to your email list. Instead of going with the generic "Sign-Up" button, however, try getting creative. A unique, contextual and action-oriented phrase such as, "I wanna join!" or "Send me my free eBook" will certainly grab your readers attention.

The Location
Your sign-up form should appear on highly-trafficked website pages, such as your homepage or blog. Ideally, you want to place it in a location where it's noticeable and grabs your visitor's attention. Since the location will also depend on the type of form you use, be sure to consider this as you decide on what form is best.

Create Incentives

People love receiving exclusive gifts and discounts. So why not add one to your sign-up form? Offering an incentive (or lead magnet) that appeals to your audience is a great way to encourage them to sign up to your email list, especially individuals who are on the fence.

Launch a Contest

Host a contest that features a valuable prize and requires an email address to enter. Promote it on social media, your website and any other place where you can interact with your audience.

Publish Value Content

People are more likely to sign up on your email list after you prove the content you have to offer is worth it. If you have a blog, take the time to write content that's going to make a difference in helping your audience.

WRITE ENGAGING EMAIL CONTENT

If having quality subscribers is one part of the equation to achieve email marketing success, then the other piece is creating valuable content. This should be the cornerstone of your email marketing strategy. After all, the only way to attract the right people to your list is by giving them content that they're interested in.

The first step? Identifying what your audience considers to be "valuable" content.

Create Engaging Content

The first step to writing email content is first identifying the value you hope to bring your subscribers. As with a branded content your audience will interact with, they will wonder what they're going to get out of it.

The answer should be clear within your email content. This crucial to creating effective emails that people not only want to sign up for, but open and engage with again and again. Remember, the more loyal that subscribers are to your emails and brand, the better it will be for your business or blog.

So how can you create emails that your subscribers want to open? Let's take a look at the different types of emails you can send, and how you can leverage each to grow your audience and business.

TYPES OF EMAILS

In the world of email marketing, there are a few different types of emails that you can send to subscribers. Each one serves a different purpose, but all are essential to every email marketing strategy.

1. Follow Up Emails
   Follow-ups (also known as autoresponders) are automated email. These are messages you can create and schedule in advance, so they automatically are sent in a sequence to those who subscribe to your email list.

2. Broadcast Emails
   A broadcast is a one-time email that is delivered to subscribers either immediately, or on a scheduled date and time. You can use a broadcast to share time-sensitive information with subscribers.

3. Email Confirmation
   The purpose of your confirmation message is to give your new subscribers a chance to confirm that they actually want to receive your emails. Maybe someone signed up accidentally, or they changed their mind.

4. Welcome Email
   As the first email your subscribers receive from you, your 'Welcome Email' should thank them for joining your list.

You should also include information on what they'll receive from you in future emails. If you offered an incentive in your sign-up form, the welcome email is the place to deliver it.

Here is a quick checklist of talking points that you'll want to include in your Welcome Email:

- Thank your subscribers
- Tell them more about your business
- Provide more information about the future email content they'll receive
- An incentive (if you offered one)
- Contact information

5. Writing Subject Lines
Want more eyes on your emails? The subject line is where to start. Think of it as the first impression you give to subscribers when your emails hit their inbox. Your emails could be filled with amazing content, but if your subject line stinks, nobody is going to read it.

6. Personalize Your Emails
Good email marketing shouldn't make people feel like they are being marketed to. They want to know that you have their best interests at heart, and that should show in the content you send them.

There are a few different ways to personalize your emails so they make your subscribers feel like you are talking directly to them, and not just one of hundreds of other people.

7. Monetize Your Emails
Email is a fantastic way to build relationships and trust with your audience. But if the goal of your emails is to make money, it can also help with that, too. Email is, hands down, the most effective channel for converting customers

compared to any other (and that includes social media and search engine marketing).

About Kokchin

Kokchin Chow is an entrepreneur and email marketing expert. He helps business owners, entrepreneurs and e-commerce brands to explode sales with email marketing automation. As an entrepreneur with farsightedness, Kokchin has helped over 100 business owners generate sales through email marketing online. Keeping pace with ever-changing world development, he is currently working in several online perspectives, specializing in "Email Marketing Automation" and lead generation.

The secret leading him to a successful path is undoubtedly related to his admirable mindset and abundant cognition towards entrepreneurship. He is a person with an ambitious attitude, willing to spend all his passion to help other businesses succeed. As a result, his strong mindset and willpower become his fuel to push him to achieve such a fruitful economic result. It is also a credit to his recognition and knowledge of the online business model and system.

More importantly, he has a worldwide vision and global connection. From numerous successful efforts in cooperation and the satisfying feedback from his clients, it has been truly revealed that he is an experienced and trustworthy expert. In the near future, he aims to provide his customers with the highest satisfying quality of service and in bridging a harmonious business relationship with every client in transactions.

You may contact Kokchin at:
- kokchin@kcchow.com
- https://www.linkedin.com/in/kokchinchow

CHAPTER 9

WHAT HAPPENED TO THE 3 MARTINI LUNCH?

BY KATIE SHUGERT

I'm envious of the guys and gals that had that 'go to' place where they'd slip out of the office and actually talk about their businesses. Some problems, some successes but always an ear to be had. Communication was slower, no immediate texts, group chats or videos. The experience relied on the face-to-face in personal meeting. They could hardly wait for the next lunch to catch up with their fellow business pals, partners, etc. on the day's or week's happenings or latest ad's response rate. Customers would give you feedback on your triumphs and failures the old fashioned way (face-to-face). No immediate social media posts blasting about a bad experience before the business even knows there was a problem.

Void of the expectations of more formal business owner and client interaction, clients felt more open about honest feedback. Sure, some still do this, but most don't. And of course lunches are still happening, but more in an employee role rather than as business owner. Sure, business owners today have tools that can streamline certain things which is great, but there's always something else to be done. That's just part of what makes an entrepreneur tick.

I'm not condoning having too many cocktails at lunch. Forget the gin and olives, being an entrepreneur can be a very lonely journey. As employees come and go, it can be frustrating and overwhelming when it seems we are the only constant in our businesses. However, as entrepreneurs we continue our relentless pursuit of solving problems and connecting all the links in the chain at the same time to see some progress and know that we did that.

As I thought about what topic I should choose to write about for this, I landed on lead generation. It's something that virtually every business must do – whether big or small. Unless you have a group of business owners you're able to confer with, it is very easy to keep doing what we're doing. Many of us are readers and obviously you are; I am not promising to provide anything truly groundbreaking, most ideas aren't. But perhaps something here will trigger a memory of something you've seen before but haven't tried, or maybe tried and didn't work. Let's face it, things are changing in this world at a very quick pace these days, and just because it didn't work 'back in the day' maybe it will today.

Since martini lunches with our fellow entrepreneurs and even customers are a thing of the past, we search for information in other ways. It is less social, but it is nonetheless an attempt to improve. These are all methods I've used. Some have worked better than others, but that partly is a reflection of our own enthusiasm for particular methods over others. Regardless, let's go through some ideas on lead generation and hopefully it will be useful to someone who reads it. If it makes a difference in one person's business, I've done my job here. The following are written from my insurance agent perspective although, as I mentioned, it can easily be utilized in other businesses.

1. Call existing clients.

When was the last time you reached out to your existing client base? You can do it or you can have your assistant or new agents do it. Just do it. Schedule annual reviews.

Life happens – marriage, divorce, babies, college, sickness, death, buying a home, selling a home. I could go on but you get the point. Call them and get in front of them for a review. Ask specific questions on your pre-made questionnaire so you don't forget anything. As long as you're not a jerk, your clients are going to enjoy seeing you and totally appreciate your thoroughness.

2. Host customer appreciation event.

If your clients are generally in one region this is an easy thing to do. Simply choose a non-offensive unbiased location for your clients to get together for, say, a barbeque. You would of course be providing the goodies as the host. Request clients to bring a friend with them. This does a couple of things:

 a) They're more likely to show up because they're not alone.
 b) You have the opportunity to be introduced to a new potential client.

If your clients are more spread out, perhaps a couple of regional events or even a virtual hangout. Be creative and think about what your clients would appreciate, enjoy or participate in the most.

3. Write an article and submit to local media offering your availability for an interview.

Make your topic both timely and relevant with a call-to-action offering a complimentary review. For example, take Baby boomers coming of age and their fear of outliving their retirement. Think of how many interesting and relevant topics you can write and speak about throughout the year. I've found it helpful to record a conversation with a friend talking about your chosen topic then transcribing that to get some material to get started. It can be a daunting thought to sit down to a blank sheet of paper or computer screen with a deadline.

4. Offer complimentary reviews to a group of which you're a member.

This is a great way to give back to a group that has helped you in your development personally or professionally. If you're good at what you do, and I'll assume that you are since you're reading this book and you've made it this far... it is your duty to take care of these people and offer your goods or services to them. I'm not saying be an overbearing, pushy salesman. I'm saying let them know what you do and how you may be able to help them.

5. Think of an underserved niche in your area of expertise and offer to bring a light snack in exchange for a few minutes speaking time.

This is just that, a few minutes, not your life story. Keep it simple, interesting and relevant to that particular group. Ahead of time, get permission to pass out cards for the group to fill out so you will have their contact info for follow up. If that's not allowed, then get permission for a sign in sheet for everyone who attends. Afterward, follow up with your group contact, asking if the information you have is helpful, then request a group roster for follow up, or even better, a recommendation of your services and roster from the group organizer.

6. Make a list of businesses you regularly do business with.

Keep in mind this works best with local businesses where you can talk to the owner face to face. Offer a complimentary review of the services you specialize in. "Hey John, I've been buying coffee here for the past three years and I have never offered my services to you. I help protect your hard earned money and make sure you don't outlive your money. It usually takes about fifteen minutes. I have some time Tuesday or Wednesday this week, which is better for you? Okay great, morning or afternoon?" It really is that simple.

7. Reach out to your attorney and accountant.

Attorneys and accountants have a lot of clients who return to them time and time again for their expertise. We rely on both to prevent and fix our people and number problems. How great would it be to get referrals from them? Set up an appointment letting them know your intention and reason for the appointment in advance, otherwise they will likely be very upset. Go through a review with them so they have a good understanding of what you do and why you do it. Then, with an attorney, say. . . "If you think any of this would be helpful to your clients with any major life change, would you be willing to refer them to me for a review like we just went through?"

With an accountant, "Any client with kids in college or paying high taxes needs a review for ways to lower their tax burden, protect money and secure it for the future."

The benefit to the attorney and accountant are higher client satisfaction, more or better quality referrals and possibly leading them to fire bad clients they don't want to work with. These are relationships that must be kept warm. Keep in touch with them. Offer to meet for coffee, drop a postcard, drop by the office (but don't expect the ability to sit down with them on a surprise pop in). It's the thought of being in their area and reaching out that's meaningful. Send a relevant article, etc. Stay top of mind with them.

8. Ask your local social butterfly for some local grassroots help.

Someone who knows everyone in your area makes all the difference. Think *Center of Influence* and ask them for introductions or to tag along to some events, parties etc.

9. **Create a YouTube video or Instagram post highlighting a common problem for your clients and a solution or possible solution.**

   The idea is for the viewer to be able to relate and that might solve a problem.

10. **Regarding existing clients:**

    When you meet with existing clients, even if you only have one, simply following the very simple rules below will lead to referrals.

    - Show up
    - Be on time
    - Behave professionally
    - Do the right thing

Yes, this is overtly obvious but often messed up especially with new employees, agents, etc., regardless of their age. Many businesses train employees on drumming up business and lead generation, others just hope they'll do it or somehow learn it through osmosis. Most won't just figure it out on their own, therefore the basics as I just mentioned are the perfect starting point regardless of their age. Yep, I mentioned it twice. Hope for the best and train for the worst. It's your business.

As I mentioned when I began this passage, some of these maybe even all of these are things you've tried before. Do more of what is working for you and try some new methods. Obviously, there are countless lead generation methods and as entrepreneurs we search for what's working now in our industries. Please don't overlook the opportunity to see what's working in other industries, and reach out to business owners with other types of businesses. When it comes down to it, it's all business. Your business isn't that different from mine or the next guy's. So be open to listening to perspectives from outside industry professionals. Books like these are great because you get snippets from professionals in all types of businesses. Take what you want and leave the rest for now. Being an entrepreneur is a journey, a fascinating never-ending journey.

About Katie

Katie Shugert is an Ohio-raised farm girl with a work ethic to prove it. She brings beauty and stability to the lives of others through insurance and real estate solutions. Her relentless pursuit of solving problems has enabled her to experience multiple industries and the highs and lows of both. She learned about real estate from her dad; looking through hundreds maybe thousands of real estate books and viewing properties while still in grade school. Growing up, Katie lived and breathed the farm. She was dedicated to her 4-H projects and was making dinner for the family starting in middle school because her mother worked 2nd shift.

Katie grew up fast, marrying at 18 while she was in college. She and her husband struggled to figure out how to survive in the cattle business and deal with the negativity that surrounded them. Sheer determination, hard work and some great timing enabled pieces to fall into place. Against all odds, they built the largest privately-owned beef cattle seedstock operation in the Eastern United States. However with the how-to of the cattle business figured out, Katie decided to go to graduate school for a new challenge. Too many moving pieces proved to be too much for a marriage of two highly ambitious and very determined individuals.

After stints at a major New York City publisher and a dark humor magazine, Katie earned her Master of Fine Arts degree but knew that was not the lifestyle she wanted. Katie and her two young children moved to upstate New York. She painted, exhibited her work, volunteered at an art gallery and simply enjoyed motherhood. After a few years, she moved back to Ohio so the children could be closer to their dad, only to be faced with a debilitating custody battle. Katie even moved in with her aunt and uncle for safety and stability *and relied on her cousin for clarity* during that time. When Katie won her case she moved to Cleveland and followed in her grandfather's steps in the insurance business.

Highly competitive and determined to succeed, Katie quickly rose to the top and was recognized as a top trainer in the world. The stress and cut-throat nature of the business took a toll on her when she found herself in the hospital for emergency surgery. The days that followed were eye-opening in many ways both personally and professionally. Passionate about her health, a self-proclaimed foodie and hot yoga fanatic, Katie believes in whole body wellness. She refuses to work with people who don't care or won't do the right thing!

Today, she works in both the insurance and real estate industries. She buys and rehabilitates single family homes to feed her soul; some of which she maintains for her own short and long term rental portfolios. Katie Shugert brings passion, understanding, enthusiasm, creativity and warmth to her agents and clients in insurance and real estate.

CHAPTER 10

LEADING OTHERS TOGREATNESS

BY BILL GRIFFIN

If you want to perform at an elevated level in business, you will need to be a great leader. There are very few situations in which you can accomplish greatness all by yourself. You will most likely need to become a great project leader, Manager, Supervisor, CEO, Entrepreneur, etc. to achieve something great. Since you are reading this, I will jump to the conclusion that you are searching for greatness or wish to accomplish something great. Greatness comes in many forms, it might be monetary success you are after or something of intrinsic value like a home or a car. Perhaps making a positive social impact is your goal.

You've got one trip around this earth; take advantage of opportunities to make an impact for yourself, your family and friends or society. In this chapter, you will find a list of important principles to achieve greatness for yourself and others. I assume that you are leading a team of employees that report directly to you or have been assigned to work with you on a project. The term employees will be used to refer to "others". However, these tips apply equally well in a variety of management, volunteer, and/or teamwork environments.

Principle #1: It's all about people—Trust, Goodwill And Balance

You may have had the misfortune of working with or for a selfish manager. It doesn't feel good to be thought of as a tool only for their betterment or benefit. If you want employees to strive for greatness you will have to tap into **their personal motivators** and discover what matters to them. To do this, you must first wipe your slate clean, or you will likely enter this with an inherent bias. You will commonly feel that your employees' wants and desires are the same as yours. Just like a snowflake is unlike any other, individual motivators vary from person to person and are impacted by the current circumstances in their lives. To learn about your employees, you must gain their trust. To gain trust, we can follow one of the principles proposed by Stephen Covey in his book, *The Speed of Trust*. If your employees believe you are acting in their best interests, they will be more likely to trust you. Learn about their interests. Find out not just what is important to them at work, but what is important to them in their lives. What do they most want to achieve, and why? It would be awesome if their interests aligned perfectly with your business goals, but that isn't likely in all cases. This doesn't mean you cannot align their interests with your business goals.

Once trust has begun to build with your employee, you should strive to add a sense of goodwill between you. Merriam Webster dictionary describes goodwill as "kindly feeling of approval and support." You are on the path to leadership when the employee trusts you and feels understood and supported by you. You must be careful to exhibit balance between personal and business goals. You must not be so supportive of their personal ambitions that you allow them to override the business goals that you have set before you. The business goals or group goals should always come first except in cases of health or welfare concern. By accomplishing goals on time, the personal rewards for you and the employee are often forthcoming. This is especially so when you and your team have a record of consistently achieving goals.

Principle #2: Don't take their monkey!

One real risk that you face as a leader is taking the monkey off the back of your employees. If you jump in and complete each task every time an employee stumbles or struggles, employees will learn your behavior and may never fully develop their own skills. By adopting this behavior, you fail your employees rather than help them. By encouraging employees to keep trying to find their path to a solution, you demonstrate confidence in their abilities. Confidence helps employees perform at a higher level and is a key component to achieving greatness. Confidence encourages risk taking, and risk taking is important to performing at the top of your game.

Confidence also plays a role in the manager's desire to jump in and solve problems as well. We all like to demonstrate our knowledge, as the accomplishment of a goal or skill feels good. It especially feels good to check items off the list that are simple for us and hard for others. I made this mistake as a new manager in my mid-twenties. I was confident my skills could improve the team, therefore I often jumped in and acted. It made sense to me that my sales team should perform tasks in the very same way. This was frustrating for both parties. I was frustrated they weren't doing things the way I expected, and they weren't any happier trying to do it my way. Looking back on myself as a new manager, I was more comfortable in my sales ability than my management skills. I relied heavily upon my sales skills to demonstrate my ability to lead. There is nothing wrong with leading from the front. In fact, it is often necessary in order to achieve greatness.

The key lesson here is: *Doing everything doesn't scale.* Eventually, I figured out how to better leverage the inherent skills and abilities of my team and let them solve their own problems. This freed up my time for the occasions where I was truly needed to make an impact. Subsequently, both manager and sales representative had greater success and we were both a lot happier with one another and our jobs.

Principle #3: Have Fun!

There is a lot of science behind the statement "people produce more when they are happy." We don't need science to tell us what we already know to be true, _but not all jobs are fun!_ If all jobs were fun, we would call it fun instead of work. Businesses and organizations cannot reach their goals by focusing solely on fun. This doesn't mean we shouldn't try as leaders to make our employee's jobs and the workplace a happy one. An example from my early adulthood applies here. I worked my way through college at a factory called Metropolitan Wire in Wilkes-Barre, Pennsylvania. My day-to-day job for over four years was on second shift as a machine operator of the "notcher". This job basically entailed picking a piece of wired steel from a conveying system, placing it in the machine, pressing two buttons simultaneously to operate the "notcher". The machine trimmed off the corner excess steel and I finally took the trimmed piece out and placed onto a dolly where it was taken for welding.

This was not fun, it was monotonous, physical and a little dangerous. Every day consisted of eight glorious hours, with two short breaks and a thirty-minute dinner break. The only way I got through those years was to set goals for myself. How many can I do in an hour? a half-day? or a full day of work? The team had a small incentive to produce more units. The incentive would range from ten to fifty-five cents per hour. Yes, the team had the possibility of earning an extra ten cents per hour if we maxed out performance as a group. This incentive was based on the group's performance, so my personal productivity had only a small impact on the productivity of a fifty-person department.

One day I was feeling particularly ambitious and worked four or five minutes into the meal period. It was very noticeable because the clanking and banging of all the other machines had stopped. The shop steward (an elected official in the Steelworkers Union) approached me as I was placing another unit in the "notcher". "What are you doing?" he said. My reply included the words "may set a record today." He looked at me like I had three eyes and said, "What the heck are you talking about?" He actually used a different word than "heck." Since there was no record to speak of, my statement simply made no sense to him.

Over my time at Metropolitan Wire Corporation, I set and broke many records. None of these were heralded, listed, or even known to anyone but me. There was, however, one particularly adept supervisor of the second shift super steel fabrication department. This manager noticed my relentless pursuit of efficiency and ever-increasing unit production and would ask me nearly every night how I did during that shift. He passed along small acknowledgments of encouragement. "Nice job" he would say, or "tomorrow the second centers machine will be up and running so we will be able to feed you more units." In truth, my individual performance didn't matter much because I was only one step in the multiple steps of the manufacturing process. My efforts always didn't go completely unrecognized by my coworkers either. Some thought my efforts made them appear to be slacking; others just looked at me furiously working and thought, "What the _ _ _ _?!!!" I didn't care as I was looking forward to a different life. I found a way to make this boring, monotonous job a little fun so that I could focus on my bigger goals: to graduate university and obtain a more rewarding career. My evening supervisor understood to some degree what drove me, and one could say he was a good manager. In truth, what this supervisor had stumbled upon is our next principle, "People Respect what you Inspect."

Principle #4:   People Respect what you Inspect

Many managers can be characterized as micromanagers. Micromanagers inspect every item as if they are all the same in importance. They spend most of their time driving their employees crazy and sapping motivation. Conversely, zero inspection points isn't the answer. As leaders we need to find the right balance. Through trial and error, I have found that the ideal number of inspection points is between three and five for any important goal. The human brain prefers to remember lists in short bursts of two, three, or four. Consider how you remember your phone number or your social security number as examples. Another tip is to arrange the first word of the goals or metrics into an acronym.

Now that you know how many items to inspect, how will you plan what to inspect? The best items to inspect are activities or milestones that lead directly to your goal. Inspecting the goal is pointless if you want to achieve greatness. *You will only know what you achieved or didn't achieve, when it is too late to do anything about it.* By breaking the goal down into manageable components or milestones, you give yourself opportunities to change the vector and reassess your progress. When a pilot flies cross-country he doesn't just go in a straight line. He is constantly changing vector due to wind currents, other flight traffic, and the dreaded turbulence. All tasks or activities are not equally critical to success; therefore, you will want to measure and inspect items that are most critical. By explaining the frequency and reasons behind the milestones and inspection items you selected, employees can jump on board and help make the correct vector choices. Getting people on board with your plan is always the best way to achieve goals, and keeping the inspection of items to a minimum allows all involved to make the correct vector choices. Make sure to put not only thought into the quantity of inspection points, but also the reasons behind their existence.

I truly hope you achieve your goals and enjoy doing so with great teams of individuals. The most enjoyment I have experienced in my career has been succeeding as part of, or in leading, teams. In terms of fun, I have come a long way since my "notcher" days. Helping others to achieve their personal goals and developing careers is where I get the most satisfaction and what I am most proud of.

About Bill

As a Partner in the consulting firm TechCXO, LLC., Bill Griffin applies enterprise level sales and leadership expertise to companies of all sizes, including startups and the mid-market. Bill's focus is on helping clients achieve their maximum revenue and operating profit potential. He validates success by helping clients achieve milestones and goals. He believes in frequent measurement and calibration of expectations and results, and you can expect a high level of personalized service and coaching from him. Bill's leadership practice focuses managers on how to get the most out of their team members via personal insight, constructive coaching and dialogue.

Throughout his career and with TechCXO, Bill has coached over ten thousand salespeople, over a thousand executive leaders and helped dozens of companies grow, scale and achieve tremendous results. He is a gifted coach and mentor who connects with people in individual sessions, workshops, corporate engagements, and keynote addresses.

Bill's experience was gained through an incredibly varied and successful career as a global sales leader, and has led large global teams in multiple functions, including Enterprise, Channels, Inside Sales, Sales Operations, Field Marketing, and Customer Success.

Among his career highlights are the following:
a. Bill started his career with Xerox Corporation where he held a variety of sales and marketing management positions of escalating responsibility.
b. Executive Vice President and Corporate officer for Aspen Technology (AZPN), a $500M provider of optimization software for the Oil/Gas and Chemical industry. Bill's global team at Aspen exceeded 700 employees in Sales (Enterprise, Channels, Inside Sales), Professional Services, and Customer Success function.
c. Bill held multiple Sales Executive positions with Autodesk (ADSK), a $3B Software firm focused on Manufacturing, Architecture, Engineering and Construction, and Media and Entertainment customers. Bill's teams at Autodesk exceeded 500 staff and held quota responsibility in excess of $2B annually. Bill's roles at Autodesk included VP Global Named Accounts, VP of Worldwide Channel Sales, and VP Global Cloud (SaaS) product sales.

Awards:

- Channel Chief: 2015, 2012 and 2011 Computer Reseller News, CRN Magazine
- Rising Star: 2010 Global Technology Distribution Council, GTDC
- Most Valuable Speaker: 2012 and 2013 Channel Focus North America and Latin America
- Kentucky Colonel: 2007 Commissioned by Governor of KY

Connect with Bill at:

- billtgriffin@linkedin.com
- bill.griffin@techcxo.com

CHAPTER 11

WHAT IF EVERYTHING YOU KNEW ABOUT VIDEO... WAS WRONG?

BY GREG ROLLETT

According to FortuneLords.com, the total number of people who use **YouTube** is now 1,300,000,000. That reads 1.3 billion, with a B.

They also state that 300 hours of video are uploaded to YouTube every minute. *Almost five billion videos are watched on YouTube every single day.* In an average month, eight out of ten 18- to 49-year-olds watch YouTube. And these stats are just for YouTube. They do not include the number of videos being uploaded and watched on Facebook or Instagram, Snapchat or on private video servers and platforms like Vimeo or Wistia.

Small businesses and entrepreneurs are still behind the eight ball and not creating enough content for the platform, especially when they need to compete with bigger, more established brands. Let's say you are a financial advisor. Someone heads onto Google or YouTube and starts searching for retirement advice. They find your YouTube account which has two videos, both filmed by your secretary on your iPhone, with no lighting or outline and talks about your firm and who you are and what products and services you offer. This is what most business owners and professionals have filmed and put online and on their websites.

Then, right next to your two homemade videos are 1,851 professionally filmed and generally helpful videos put on YouTube by Dave Ramsey. Instead of just telling people who he is and what products he wants to sell you, he has videos that address the needs and problems of his market. He addresses them in a fun, engaging and entertaining way.

His videos are titled: *The Secret to Not Being Broke, How to Get Out of Debt* and *The Truth About Financial Infidelity.* Yours is titled: *How to Work with Jim Smith Financial.*

Which expert is more helpful for someone looking for financial advice? Who builds more trust with their audience? Who has more authority and positioning within the market? The answer is obvious. Yet so many business owners and entrepreneurs will complain that video just doesn't work for them, or for that matter, any marketing whatsoever.

But this is what you were taught. This is what you were told to do. You were told to just film a video and put it online. You were told to use that great smartphone that's in your pocket to film your videos. You were told that camera was just as good or better than a point-and-shoot camera from the electronics store.

But it's not. And your content is not good enough to break through the noise. So how do you break through and get a piece of the billion plus views happening online every day?

Some of the BIG Questions you need to ask yourself right now are:

(A). WHAT IF EVERYTHING YOU WERE TOLD ABOUT USING ONLINE VIDEO TO GET NEW CLIENTS...WAS WRONG?

Just because someone is telling you about a brand-new trend or that you have to do something, doesn't mean that you should do it. In the case of online video, you not only shouldn't do it, but it needs to be at the top of your list. You already saw that billions (not millions but billions) of videos are being played on YouTube every single day. Add billions more on Facebook and you can really start to see where consumer behavior and attention is going.

This is how we spend our time today. We spend it watching videos on platforms like YouTube and Facebook and we do it every free minute in our schedule, whether that is waiting in line at the supermarket or in between calls at the office.

Your job as a business owner is to effectively generate the attention of people who need your services. The best and most effective way to do that is through video. But not just any kind of video, as you can see with the Dave Ramsey example above.

When putting videos online, you need to directly reach and speak to your market. And you need to do it in a way that makes you and your business appealing to them, otherwise your video will be seen for mere seconds before a viewer clicks onto the next one. You need the right approach to video marketing or else your videos will merely just be the noise that clutters up our Newsfeeds, instead of helping you to get clients and customers.

(B). WHAT IF YOUR SMARTPHONE IS NOT THE BEST CAMERA TO USE TO CREATE CLIENT-GETTING VIDEOS?

We all have cameras in our pockets and in our hands. This one device has changed everything about how we communicate with each other. Whether it's instant access to social networks, taking photos of our food, texting emoji's to our friends, parents and bosses, or actually calling someone, we have an all-powerful communication system in our pockets.

The data also shows that we are spending a lot of time on that mobile device watching video. The analytics firm Flurry, says that the average person spends five hours on their phone every single day. They also stated that 51% of those five hours are spent watching video or consuming media.

Your phone is the greatest content-consumption device ever created. But just because you and your market are watching video on your smartphone doesn't mean you should be creating video content with it.

Case in point: I'm sure you've seen someone filming a video for Facebook Live or just posting a video to social media that was filmed in selfie mode. For those unaware, selfie mode is when you turn the camera to face you and not out towards the world. This causes many issues in video production. First, most of us are not trained cinematographers and have no concept of lighting, backgrounds or environment. This leads to video with bad lighting, bad sound and McDonald's wrappers in the background. All of this is bad when it comes to producing videos to get clients.

And that's just the start. Add in the concept of angles and where you hold the camera and you can end up with a double chin, an exposed forehead or people seeing way too much of what you have going on in your nostrils. This happens because whatever is closest to the camera appears the biggest. If you hold your phone over your head, pointing down, your forehead will appear larger than it is in reality. If you hold it down and facing up, you get the double chin or the exposed nostrils. Add in poor sound, wind and shaky hand syndrome and you will quickly find out that people do not want to tune in to your videos.

So remember, even though you have a video camera in your pockets, you might want to think twice before you try and use it to get clients.

(C). WHAT IF YOU DON'T NEED TO FLY OUT TO HOLLYWOOD TO GET THE WORLD'S BEST VIDEO TEAM?

Now that you know your smartphone is not the best video studio for you to use to film client-getting videos, you might be thinking that you need to book your flight to Hollywood and go all out on a full-scale video production.

Here's the truth: almost all good video guys today can point the camera at you and make you look decent in an online video or TV show. What the average (or even above average) video guys don't know is the marketing side. They don't know how you will use the video, what platform it's going on, how your prospects and market will interact with it, how to get their attention and film the video so that after your prospects watch it, they will take action and want to work with you.

This is the missing link in so many videos. Even if your video looks great and is produced at a high level, it likely will never convert because it's essentially a brochure in video format. This is not what is going to help you grow your business.

The reason we do episodic online TV shows for our clients is that each episode is crafted as a hook to get the attention of your market. Each episode is meant to tug at their emotions, question their beliefs and make them understand that they need help to solve their problem. And you are the solution. Every episode includes a call-to-action and next steps, in addition to genuinely helping your audience to get informed and educated.

You don't need a Hollywood budget to do this. You need someone that thinks like a marketer.

(D). WHAT IF YOU DIDN'T CRAM EVERYTHING YOU DO INTO ONE 10-MINUTE VIDEO?

I love the ads that used to appear in the Yellow Pages when I was studying marketing in school. The ads would have a photo of an attorney and an 800 number and all around him in bright bubble letters were all of the specialty areas for which that firm could potentially help you. He was not only a bail bondsman, but a bankruptcy attorney, a family law attorney and a personal injury specialist.

This is not how you want to come across in your online TV show. If someone can't quickly identify how you can help them, they will not call you to help them. You need to be the definitive expert in your market, not a jack of all trades.

One of the best marketing lessons that has stayed with me
for decades now is that:
"A confused mind won't buy."

When you try to cram everything you do into one video, you leave your audience confused. This audience will never convert into a client, no matter how hard you try. We film episodic online TV for our clients, because every week we can hyper-focus on one topic. We can go deep and showcase our subject matter expertise in 3-6 minutes. At the end of the episode, the viewer is explained a problem, taught the solution and shown that you are the expert that can help deliver a solution.

This is the most important thing to remember if you are trying to use online video to get clients. You're not trying to do too much. You are trying to show the world that you are the most uniquely qualified person on the planet to help deliver a specific result to your market. Remember this over time as you go to shoot a video. Ask yourself, "Why am I shooting this video?" That will ensure that you hit your target every time.

(E). WHAT IF YOU DIDN'T HAVE TO GO VIRAL TO GROW YOUR BANK ACCOUNT?

We all want to go viral. I would be straight up lying to you if I told you I didn't want millions of people to see my videos. And we do have videos with hundreds of thousands of views.

However, the majority of my videos are seen by only a few hundred to a few thousand people. Even though these numbers are not gigantic or newsworthy, they have provided me the ability and the good fortune to build an incredible business and fuel my life with my family. We vastly overestimate the number of people we actually need to reach in order to make a great living. This isn't to say that we don't want to reach more people. It's not about quantity, it's about quality. Not everyone in your community needs your help. You need to show your videos and TV shows to the people that are most likely to hire you and buy your services.

The good news is that through platforms like Facebook and YouTube you can advertise your video to the exact people that match your perfect prospect profile. Many times you can pay these companies mere pennies to show your episode to that perfect prospect. This is an incredible way to make an impact without having to pay for the people who cannot or do not have the means to utilize your unique gifts and talents.

No matter what the next guru or expert is peddling to you about video and getting millions of viral views, be proud that your video actually made a difference in the lives of the people who see it, and that your business keeps getting bigger every time you put out a new episode.

(F). HOW MANY VIDEO MARKETING MISTAKES ARE YOU MAKING IN YOUR BUSINESS?

For starters, if you are not filming regular, consistent video content, in the form of an online TV show for Facebook and

YouTube, you are making the biggest mistake of all. This is not something to plan for in the future or when you get to it. This is the here and now. I don't want you and your great business to go the way of Blockbuster video and virtually disappear overnight because you didn't adapt and change.

The opportunity is staring at you, but it's up to you to use the ideas posed by the big questions in this chapter. Do it correctly and you will get the short term benefit of new clients and business and the long-term effects of brand building that can only be done by constantly and consistently pushing out new episodes of your online TV show.

I cannot wait to see what you do with online video to grow your business.

[Reprint of Greg Rollett's chapter in the best-selling book, *The Big Question*.]

About Greg

Greg Rollett is an Emmy Award-Winning Producer, Best-Selling Author and Marketing Expert who works with experts, authors and entrepreneurs all over the world. He utilizes the power of new media, direct response and personality-driven marketing to attract more clients and to create more freedom in the businesses and lives of his clients.

After creating a successful string of his own educational products and businesses, Greg began helping others in the production and marketing of their own products and services.

Greg has written for *Mashable, Fast Company, Inc.com, the Huffington Post, AOL, AMEX's Open Forum* and others, and continues to share his message helping experts and entrepreneurs grow their business through marketing. He has co-authored best-selling books with Jack Canfield, Dan Kennedy, Brian Tracy, Tom Hopkins, James Malinchak, Robert Allen, Ryan Lee and many other leading experts from around the world.

Greg's client list includes Michael Gerber, Brian Tracy, Tom Hopkins, Sally Hogshead, Coca-Cola, Miller Lite and Warner Brothers, along with thousands of entrepreneurs and small-business owners across the world. Greg's work has been featured on FOX News, ABC, NBC, CBS, CNN, *USA Today, Inc.* magazine, *Fast Company, The Wall Street Journal, The Daily Buzz* and more.

To contact Greg, please visit:
- http://ambitious.com
- greg@ambitious.com

CPSIA information can be obtained
at www.ICGtesting.com
Printed in the USA
LVHW081834170419
614531LV00011B/189/P